LEADING
BY EXAMPLE

LEADING
BY EXAMPLE

How We Can Inspire an Energy
and Security Revolution

BILL RICHARDSON

John Wiley & Sons, Inc.

Published by John Wiley & Sons, Inc., Hoboken, New Jersey
Published simultaneously in Canada

Wiley Bicentennial Logo: Richard J. Pacifico

Design and composition by Navta Associates, Inc.

For general information about our other products and services, please contact our Customer Care Department within the United States at (800) 762-2974, outside the United States at (317) 572-3993 or fax (317) 572-4002.

Wiley also publishes its books in a variety of electronic formats. Some content that appears in print may not be available in electronic books. For more information about Wiley products, visit our web site at www.wiley.com.

Library of Congress Cataloging-in-Publication Data:

Richardson, Bill, date.
    Leading by example : how we can inspire an energy and security revolution / Bill Richardson.
        p. cm.
    Includes index.
    ISBN 978-0-470-18637-4 (cloth)
    1. Energy policy—United States. 2. Power resources—Government policy—United States. I. Title.
    HD9502.U52R49 2008
    333.790973—dc22
                                                                    2007029108

Printed in the United States of America

10 9 8 7 6 5 4 3 2 1

To Barbara, for her ideas, for her support over decades of dedicated public service, and for letting me try to be the leader America needs.

This book is further dedicated to the American people, whose enthusiastic attention and commitment will be necessary to meet the nation's energy, security, and climate challenges in the decade ahead.

We have learned that we cannot live alone, at peace; that our own well-being is dependent on the well-being of other nations far away. We have learned that we must live as [people], and not as ostriches, nor as dogs in the manger. We have learned to be citizens of the world, members of the human community.

—*Franklin D. Roosevelt, January 1945*

The new Frontier of which I speak is not a set of promises—it is a set of challenges. It sums up not what I intend to offer the American people, but what I intend to ask of them.

—*John F. Kennedy, July 1960*

CONTENTS

Introduction

M ost Americans grow up believing that their country is great—not perfect, but a model for other nations. The United States is where anyone can achieve almost anything, depending on how hard he or she is willing to work. It is a nation where ideals such as freedom and democracy are vigorously discussed and defended every day.

That greatness will help us meet the single largest challenge we face as a nation today: our energy, security, and climate policies have left us far too heavily dependent on foreign oil, and on fossil fuels in general. The results include overexposure to price spikes that badly hurt people and the economy, vulnerability to hostile nations and terrorists, and a carbon-clogged atmosphere with the prospect of catastrophic climate change that could change Earth as we know it, potentially affecting billions of human lives.

Public concern is provoked daily by the high gasoline prices forcing everyday folks to spend more money on transportation costs instead of on household equity, education, or health expenses. There are larger, hidden costs as well. Our trade deficit suffers from our purchases of foreign oil, affecting borrowing costs and long-range prospects for investment and growth in our economy. We defend oil around the world at great cost, and we will need to spend much more on reacting and adapting if climate change is allowed to gain momentum.

By quickly adopting and implementing the policies I recommend in this book, we can do much better. We can stop paying hundreds of billions of petrodollars every year to oil-producing countries and use that money to rebuild manufacturing and opportunity across the United States. The price of change will not be very high, and it is far lower than the costs of continuing what we have been doing.

This book is my effort to show the nation, no matter who is the next president, what needs to be done. We need a national effort, led by an enthusiastic and informed president, to bring Congress, the public, and business together behind this important national mission.

Some of what I say in these pages will be controversial. I am particularly rough on the leaders in the White House and Congress who have watched the energy situation dramatically worsen in the past six or seven years, yet have not offered even the ghost of a program to change direction. My criticisms of past congresses are aimed not at Republicans or Democrats but at those who continue—regardless of who's in charge—to stand in the way of needed energy and climate policy. Further, my focus on the president is meant not to be partisan, because energy and climate are not a partisan issue, but instead to indicate his failure to address these huge issues. (I know many Republicans who are as distraught about the lack of leadership on these issues as I have been.) I am also hard on a few players in the existing energy and auto industries. I don't take the doctrinal line professed by many energy advocates, from environmentalists to libertarians. Instead, I mix a lot of needed initiatives into a comprehensive, integrated program that will produce results quickly. We need to be honest about people's interests and their potential to be involved in new solutions. But at the end of the day, we also need to work together to meet these challenges comprehensively and quickly.

I don't provide much fluffy rhetoric in this book. I leave that to other candidates. This book is about real issues facing the country, issues that desperately demand forceful and focused attention. I am willing to gore some oxen, because I know there can be no sacred cows. I try to provide solutions, not just describe problems. Sometimes it may seem that I talk more about old options (like coal) than about new ones (like solar). That's because we are more than 50 percent dependent on coal for electricity today, a situation that is both dangerous for the atmosphere and a bad model for the developing world. And I include some personal stories to keep it from being too wonky. Policy shouldn't be painful!

As you'll see, I believe we must act boldly, and we must act now. I am not proposing half measures or long-term solutions. I want to reduce oil dependence by 50 percent by 2020, and I want to reduce carbon emissions sharply and quickly so that we are down 20 to 30 percent by 2020 and 90 percent by 2050. And I expect that after enacting our domestic program, we will be in position to lead the world again—to be great again, the way Americans know we, and our nation, were born to be.

CHAPTER 1

No Challenge Is Greater or More Important

S everal years ago, I had a visit from some oil executives in my Santa Fe office that signaled sharp, surprising, sudden changes in world energy markets.

The executives told me a story, a rather frightening story, about a liquefied natural gas (LNG) tanker that had been en route to the United States only the week before, carrying a load of natural gas under contract to a buyer in the United States.

The tanker had turned around, literally done a 180, when buyers in Asia decided to intercept that natural gas on its way to markets in the United States by paying the contract penalties and a price premium.

I don't know whether it was day or night, stormy or quiet, but picture it: the diversion of a huge tanker carrying liquefied natural gas, out on the high seas. The order comes in. The tanker turns around. In a relatively stable, long-term market like that for natural gas, this was a big event. For a buyer to turn a huge LNG tanker around, and for U.S. buyers to face such unpredictable competition, marks a significantly new world.

Oil and gas markets are tightening. Global pressures from the explosion of economic growth in China and India are changing world oil and gas supply and demand, perhaps structurally. As a result, prices are higher than we expected they could ever reach. The price of oil broke through $70 per barrel in July 2007, even as the U.S. Senate passed a relatively toothless energy bill that does too little too late. (And that bill—with nothing to address climate change, renewable electricity mandates, or new incentives for alternative energy—still needs to clear several hurdles to become law.)

Gasoline costs are around three dollars a gallon. People can't afford these prices and the other everyday costs of living. Some are forced to make choices—bad choices between putting food on the table and getting to work, paying medical bills and staying warm, building their equity through education and filling the tank.

Meanwhile, the world's climate is starting to change around us. We humans have burned so much fossil energy that the atmosphere of the world we live in is warming. The results could be Earth-changing and hugely disruptive if we don't quickly change our energy technologies and fuels.

The executives who told me the LNG tanker story wanted my support for more oil and gas production in the United States, especially in New Mexico, where I have instituted new environmental controls and supported the protection of ecologically sensitive areas treasured by hunters, ranchers, and conservationists.

But my reaction was different. I know we're hooked on oil and gas, and I know that producing more and more won't cure that addiction. We should leave some resources in place for future generations, and we need a quick, decisive shift away from the energy policies that have put us where we are today.

Hearing that story further convinced me that we aren't doing nearly enough to create energy efficiency, to use renewable energy, to get new technologies into the marketplace so that our energy markets feature competition and choice. Seeing the energy legislation working through a divided Congress convinces me that the people making policy in Washington aren't acting boldly enough, by a long measure. Meeting people around the country on my presidential campaign travels convinces me that Americans want large changes that will bring down energy costs over time, create jobs in the United States, strengthen our national security, and protect the climate. The world is waiting.

I am confident about our nation's ability to address the energy challenge, but there is no question that the next president of the United States must provide the leadership to change our energy, security, and climate policies—or else. The country, even the world, can't afford to stay on the energy path we have taken. It directly threatens our national interests and undermines our national security, and it is a path we have returned to again and again over the past thirty years despite embargoes, trade deficits, wars, and price shocks.

I am not only confident in our nation's ability to address this energy challenge, I am also fully optimistic about it. This is a great opportunity for America. It is a time for optimism and positive ideas, not for pessimism and bowed heads.

Energy issues are big issues. They are all-encompassing. Every time a middle- or lower-income American pulls up to the gas pump, energy issues hit hard—right in the wallet. And these issues stretch all the way from the wallet to the atmosphere, where our global overdependence on fossil fuels clogs the climate with carbon dioxide, leading to global warming.

Our nation's dependence on oil threatens everything we care about, everything from our economy and environment to our national security to our atmosphere. Our dependence on oil creates targets for terrorists and other threats to our national security, from nuclear weapons to economic uncertainty. The states—including New Mexico, the "clean-energy state"—have done a lot to address the oil dependency challenge, but the federal government must be engaged at a far more intense level. We have become so dependent on oil because of our nation's failure to implement needed energy alternatives, from efficiency to clean cars to renewable energy.

Over recent years the price of oil has averaged about five times as high as it was when it bottomed out in the late 1990s. Now, in 2007, the price is about seven times what it was back then. As U.S. energy secretary from 1998 to 2001, I found that there was little appetite for alternatives when the price of oil went down to nine or ten dollars a barrel. Today, we see the error of our ways. The continuing petroleum price pendulum swings appear to catch us by surprise, even though for the past thirty years that same pendulum has been swinging in both directions, and hurting us badly when it swings the wrong way. Because the energy issue is so critical, we need to approach it with a much more focused and higher-priority campaign.

We need stability, diversity, competition, and sustainability in our energy supplies and energy technologies and practices. When oil is cheap, we seem to forget about the need to change. We can't afford a long-range campaign to get off oil, and we can't afford feel-good policies, because long-range and feel-good are how we got where we are today. And "today" includes 65 percent dependence on foreign oil, high energy prices, almost total reliance on fossil fuels (especially for transportation), and increasing climate pollution.

The reason I am optimistic and confident that we can change is that the technologies are available for us to do so. Further, we are already spending so much on energy that we will actually save money by converting our energy markets. Above all, however, the American people want change and they are enthusiastic about it. Everywhere I go, I encounter students, senior citizens, business people, scientists, entrepreneurs, inventors, factory workers, teachers—real people who want real change.

We're ready! We have seen enough to know that gradual, partial solutions don't work. We know that the sensible solutions are renewable and sustainable. We want to preserve Earth for future generations, not pollute it, warm it, drill it to death. We know we can make the necessary changes. We just need the program and the leadership.

Acting quickly, because of the threat to our role in the world and our national and economic security, is the core of the energy and climate policies I suggest in this book and have been talking about on the presidential campaign trail. "Go slow" makes sense in some contexts, but it absolutely does not in the area of energy policy.

The temptation to slack off, to dither, to backslide, to linger in pleasant side channels is too great when our nation starts on a multidecade campaign. This energy policy needs to get going right now. It needs sharp, intense investment and policy change. It needs to be sustained at a high level of intensity for five to ten years. This will produce results, and quickly.

When John F. Kennedy asked Americans to reach out for the Moon, he didn't say that we should take forty years to do it. He said he wanted to do it in ten years. That's why I say that the analogy between man on the Moon and energy policies, as offered by many elected officials today, is cheap unless it's based on a commitment to act fast.

JFK based his call to action on his concern for national security—that Soviet Russia would control space after its successful and surprising launch of Sputnik in 1957. JFK's program required national will, national focus, and bipartisan cooperation. We succeeded in meeting JFK's challenge less than ten years later, in 1969. We succeeded because we changed direction, invested, and focused ourselves on a central goal. We didn't patter back and forth from year to year saying, well, this year we need a booster rocket. Or this year, let's send an astronaut up in the air to orbit Earth. And this year, we need to send an unmanned ship to orbit or land on the Moon. Instead we made a plan, supported by clear implementation measures, to achieve a goal, and we achieved it. The intermediate steps were necessary, but they were recognized as intermediate.

There's another great example of national determination and national leadership that addressed a major security threat quickly. When Franklin D. Roosevelt brought the United States into World War II following the attack at Pearl Harbor, he did it intensely. He did it based on a clear and present danger to national security. With the cooperation of Congress and the almost unanimous support of the American people, FDR launched a single-minded campaign to enter and win a world war. Within four years, our involvement in the war had turned the tables, and both Nazi Germany and Hirohito's Japan had surrendered to Allied forces.

My view is that our oil dependence is a great threat to the national security of the United States. Everything we do, including war, requires oil, and the shadow of oil lies across many of our international challenges. When we invaded Iraq, securing its oil fields was at the top of our list. When we wrangle with Iran over its nascent nuclear program, we are arguing with a nation whose ability to conduct nuclear programs derives from its oil wealth. When we discuss the spread of democracy with unsympathetic leaders from oil-rich nations, we know that they have the autonomy that comes with owning oil. When we fight terrorists, we often fight against people and movements who are directly or indirectly funded by our own petrodollars.

No challenge is greater or more important than gaining energy security and addressing threats to Earth as a whole. But my approach is to be candid about our challenges without saying that the sky is falling. (Today Chicken Little might have a different approach, saying the sky is warming—and she'd be right.) We should recognize the mistakes we have made getting to where we are. I particularly fault the president and Congress for their failure to act responsibly in recent years, and credit the states, cities, and other nations who have worked hard to reverse direction on energy and climate issues.

The American people don't need or deserve scolding. They are ready to change. They want a better future. And they see possibility and opportunity—not the grim and fearful scenarios painted by those who do not accept the idea that we need to change. It's time to move the obstacles out of the way and forge an energy future that serves and protects our interests. That's the challenge before us.

CHAPTER 2

1997–2007: Then and Now

T en years make a decade. They also make a difference, especially in energy and security policy.

Ten years ago I was the United States Ambassador to the United Nations. I had just left my seat in Congress, after about fifteen years as a member of the House Energy and Commerce Committee. When I came to the United Nations, I saw an opportunity to help President Bill Clinton with his strong vision for international cooperation and U.S. leadership in a world increasingly trending toward democracy and human rights (despite some obvious exceptions).

President Clinton's general principles on world affairs earned him enormous respect around the globe. He was seen as both a leader and a team player. The vision of stable nations working together to bring peace to troubled nations seemed to be within our grasp. It appeared that we had the tools—we only needed to get better at wielding them. The United States was respected around the world, and working at the United Nations meant making new friends—not new enemies, as we seem to have done in more recent years—in our concerted program to maintain world peace, protect human rights, and support civil government around the world, while diligently protecting U.S. interests.

I was excited about the opportunity to use my background in foreign affairs, energy, and Congress to support President Clinton's international program. When he called in late 1996 to offer me the post, just after his overwhelming reelection, I needed about two seconds to think it over. Working at the United Nations was definitely something I wanted to do for the president, the United States, and myself.

At that time, in early 1997, oil prices were under $20 a barrel. They didn't stay there. I remember an article in *Business Week* titled "The New Economics of Oil" in the fall of 1997. The content of that article seems quaint today. What we then considered earth-shaking was clearly, in the cold, retrospective light of 2007, a modest tremor compared to what we have experienced since. The article pointed out that "the threat of armed conflict between Iran and Iraq sent crude prices soaring from $20 a barrel to almost $23" in early October 1997. ("Soaring" more aptly describes what has happened to oil prices in more recent years.)

Back in 1997, we saw a sudden, unexpected two- to three-dollar-a-barrel change in oil prices as a signal of volatility and distortion in oil markets. Today that kind of fluctuation can occur daily, as a matter of course.

Business Week went further. After noting the sudden change in oil prices, stimulated as it so often is by turmoil in the Middle East, the article stated, "Even as the world is reminded of the vulnerability of its oil supply, consumption is soaring. Americans have fallen in love with gas guzzlers such as the Ford Expedition." There's that word "soaring" again. Consumption was soaring as the price of oil went higher.

For many Americans in 1997, the Ford Expedition SUV and its competitors meant safety, comfort, and modern convenience. Now they signify pain at the pump. The SUV has become an icon of our energy problems in the United States. Cartoons lampoon them. Radicals burn them in car sale lots. People shake their fists at them and gloat when they see their owners frowning at the gas pumps. The SUV phenomenon deserves a few words.

I personally like a sport utility vehicle. I'm a big guy, and I don't really fit well in smaller cars. I usually travel with security agents and staff. For a while we used the largest hybrid we could find, an Escape that Ford executives bent over backward to get for me in a tight market a few years ago. It turned out to be too small for me, my state security staff, and one or two of my people, so now we use larger SUVs that can hold more people.

We try to make sure they are "flex-fuel" compatible, meaning that they can use 85-percent nonpetroleum-based, renewable ethanol fuels (E-85), and in New Mexico—where we have only a few pumps providing that kind of fuel—we fill the tank with E-85 whenever we can.

Ralph Nader sent me an angry letter about my driving habits and choice of vehicle a few years ago. I think he wanted me to downsize. I couldn't if I wanted to get my job done. The reality was that my downsizing would just result in another police car and staff driving separately, creating more environmental impact than the SUV alone. The same dynamic affects some other SUV users.

I recognize that a lot of families and other users want extra size in their vehicles. So I do not categorically condemn all SUVs. I'm not going to demonize their owners and say that everyone needs to trade down to a fuel-efficient compact car. Farmers, ranchers, contractors, and large families sometimes need them. Others simply prefer them.

However, I have called on Americans to make some sacrifices to break our dependence on oil, and I know many Americans can safely and comfortably use smaller cars. Some can help build markets for renewable fuels by fueling up on E-85 instead of straight gasoline. Some can buy diesels—generally about 20 to 30 percent more efficient and increasingly clean compared to the older diesels. As hybrid and plug-in models become more available, SUV owners should give them a fair shake.

I hope SUV owners will also stay open to the concept of lightening their vehicles. We don't need ten thousand pounds of metal and glass around us to be safe. To achieve better fuel economy, SUVs need to incorporate much lighter materials that are proven safe and strong. People need to be willing to change if we are going to meet these daunting energy and climate challenges.

We can achieve far better fuel efficiency and develop alternative fuel-saving technologies. We need a wide variety of fuel-efficient cars to appeal to every kind of driver. In 2007, Chrysler announced a high-powered, muscular hybrid hemi (their most powerful engine)—a step in the right direction.

In 1997, low gas prices fueled the boom in big cars, and there was no end in sight. Congress, a shortsighted institution by nature, didn't support higher fuel efficiency standards. Detroit auto manufacturers put all their eggs in the conventional SUV basket and left hybrid technology innovation and fuel efficiency entirely to the Japanese. At that point, the future of oil prices and supply and demand was opaque.

The *Business Week* article ended with the oil-price equivalent of saying "It won't rain today, so forget the umbrella." Everyone knows that it rains the hardest on the days you leave the umbrella at home. It said, firmly, that the improving technology to bring oil in from new frontiers would forever preserve supply, even against rapidly growing demand: "War and politics aside, technology is the driving force in the oil industry today. And although nature gave us only so much oil, technology will pull more from the ground than people ever dreamed possible."

It wasn't hubris to make that kind of statement, because technology does deliver. As I say time and again, the twenty-first century is going to be ruled by geeks, and no one's geeks are smarter than ours. (I might have read that in one of Tom Friedman's *New York Times* columns or in his book *The World Is Flat*.) Technology is going to play a huge role in the U.S. response to the energy and climate crisis facing our nation and the world. Yet a technology-starstruck statement like *Business Week*'s was too optimistic. In 1997 the Asian economy was in an especially stagnant condition, and the prediction that we'd always have enough oil did not acknowledge the additional oil needs of large developing economies such as China's and India's.

In retrospect, the 1997 brush with higher oil prices and volatility in international oil markets should have alerted us to a huge problem. Not only had we abandoned our sensible energy independence goals, we had grown accustomed to making energy policy on a year-to-year reactive basis, instead of setting a course and sticking to it. We have allowed energy policy to be driven by the demands of the energy industry rather than by the broader interests of the United States and its people.

It was during 1997 that Toyota rolled out its Prius gasoline-powered hybrid vehicle, at least in Japan. (The Prius took three more years to reach showrooms in the United States, arriving in 2000.) At the same time that Detroit was producing cars that consumed even more gas, Japanese automakers were developing and marketing highly efficient products that were models of new technology. And they didn't do it based on a bad year for oil prices. Developing and rolling out the Prius was a process that took several years. In contrast, the major innovation in the United States in 1997 might have been the institution of inter-league games in professional baseball.

Historians and political scientists often say you can't see his-tory until after it happens. In other words, we don't know what is important until we have some perspective. Toyota's decision to lock down its position as an international marketer of highly effi-cient vehicles played at least some role in the fact that 2007 marks Toyota's ascension to world supremacy as the top-selling auto producer, finally ahead of General Motors and far ahead of Ford, which has been slipping fast.

Toyota thought ten years ahead of its competitors, and ten years later, it has won this round.

"Move Over G.M., Toyota Is No. 1" read the business-page headline in the *New York Times* on April 25, 2007. American dominance of the auto markets was relinquished, at least for now, to Japanese automakers that have excelled in producing smaller, more efficient cars. And with the tripling of oil prices since early 1997—prices that are higher than anyone had expected and are staying high, unlike previous price spikes—Toyota finally made its leap to the top. The news that Toyota is number one is sad tid-ings for hundreds of thousands of auto workers and their families in communities that support the American auto industry. Although Japanese carmakers have built great factories here using American labor, we all want to see the American industry thrive and grow—which I believe will happen again if my pro-posals in this book are followed.

The Prius is not a technological marvel. It simply marries

electric battery technology with conventional gasoline engine technology. The car saves fuel by running on electric power (the batteries) when the battery has enough power to do so. The gasoline engine, which charges the battery, is less efficient in stop-and-go conditions (which is why the national mileage numbers for conventional cars always show better gas mileage for highway than for city driving).

When you take your foot off the gas in a conventional car and apply the brakes, you are using the engine to supply stopping power even as the engine and transmission are still trying to move forward. In contrast, when you take your foot off the accelerator in a plug-in or a gasoline-electric hybrid vehicle, you instantly stop generating forward momentum, and you can use the force of the brakes to create more electrical energy, which goes back into the batteries. This basic difference is one of the reasons that plug-in and hybrid autos are more efficient than conventional gasoline engines.

Unlike conventionally powered cars, hybrids generally get better gas mileage in city driving than they do on the highway because the battery power is so much more efficient for stop-and-go driving. It's only when the gasoline engine kicks in for longer-distance driving that mileage begins to drop.

Hybrid vehicles shouldn't be confused with hydrogen vehicles. Toyota brought its hydrogen-powered Highlander to Santa Fe in 2004, and they let me take a spin. I hadn't driven in a couple of years, because the state security team usually drives me around. So I was a little nervous when, taking the driver's seat, I was informed that the vehicle was worth $3 million, or some such astronomical amount. It had all kinds of fancy technology on board, from hydrogen storage to the hydrogen fuel cell. Toyota's officials gasped when I drove away from the state capitol and, in front of the media and my security team, turned the wrong way onto the one-way street at the end of the capitol drive-way. Quickly realizing my mistake, I got the $3 million car going in the right direction, and everybody and everything, including the $3 million car and the governor behind the wheel, was safe and sound.

We all had a good laugh, and the reporters got a good story.

But there's a metaphor in there, as well: it would be all too easy for our political leaders to take us in the wrong direction, and hydrogen cars are, for now, the wrong direction. Hydrogen vehicles aren't quite ready for market, owing to all the expensive and as yet imperfect technology, as well as the demand for a whole new transportation infrastructure to produce, refine, trans-port, store, and sell hydrogen. They're a thirty-year solution to a five-year problem. That's why my own view is that the president and others should quit talking about the hydrogen car and instead emphasize new gas-saving technologies that could be in the market within a few years. The time will come for hydrogen, but plug-in and hybrid vehicles are a first step toward needed short-term progress.

(A quick note about "plug-in" vehicles: There are two kinds. The first is the pure plug-in that runs only from electricity taken from your wall outlet or another electricity source. The second is a hybrid, like the gasoline-electric hybrids such as the Prius, except that it can also be plugged into the wall. Whereas today's Prius runs only on gasoline, either directly or to charge up its batteries, the plug-in hybrid can run on either gasoline or elec-tricity from the marketplace, giving the consumer new range and choice.)

In 1997, for most Americans, the idea of hybrid gasoline-electric cars or hydrogen cars seemed about as likely to catch on as jet packs or personal spaceships. And yet, ten years later, Amer-icans have accepted gasoline-hybrid technology with open arms.

Tax incentives have helped, but the largest incentive has been the rising price of gasoline.

Sometimes, when I talk about changing the way we think about energy and adopting new technologies, I can see that people think I'm talking pie-in-the-sky politics. But I'm not. I'm not that kind of guy. The Prius is a good example of something that sounded like science fiction one day and was commonly accepted the next. Plug-in cars, which should be the next big step for automotive technology, as I will discuss in chapter 8, are ready for market now too.

New automobile technologies such as gasoline-electric hybrids were largely dismissed as "fringe" a decade ago. U.S. automakers ceded the markets for these vehicles to Japanese and European automakers because they thought consumer acceptance in the United States would be minimal. Detroit also believed that the price of gasoline would stay relatively affordable for the longer term. And it knew that the United States would never adopt gasoline taxes like those in Europe, where the taxes can double the price. U.S. automakers believed that hybrid and diesel vehicles were more suited to those overseas markets, where consumers don't consider purchasing larger, American-style vehicles. For the longer term, they were wrong.

Those were the conditions and that was the thinking in 1997. We didn't realize that we were getting a glimpse of something much bigger, that we were seeing only the tip of the oil-price iceberg. We weren't clairvoyant. I had no inkling, either, that I would be named energy secretary a year later. Like other Americans, I watched the price volatility affecting international oil markets and wondered where it would lead, but I had no idea I would end up running the Department of Energy during perhaps the most volatile, up-and-down period for oil prices in world history. There were other issues demanding my (and the world's) attention at the United Nations, including Saddam Hussein's refusal to cooperate with international weapons inspections. There was also a huge change happening in the underworld of international terrorism—which is connected to the energy issue. The price of oil wasn't the only major signal we didn't understand ten years ago.

In 1997, Osama bin Laden settled into his new base of operations in Kandahar, Afghanistan, with the protection of that nation's Taliban fundamentalist government.

Before that, for most of the 1990s, he'd been in Sudan, where he'd built a substantial financial and physical network. In the mid-1990s, knowing that bin Laden was an international threat and particularly hostile to the United States, the Clinton administration started putting serious pressure on Sudan to hand him over. (Within a couple of years we bombed Al Qaeda facilities in Sudan.) Eventually, bin Laden fled Sudan for Afghanistan, knowing that its rulers, the Taliban, would never turn him over.

Throughout 1997, he consolidated his power in Afghanistan, using Taliban resources to bolster his forces and laying the groundwork for bombings (embassies and the USS *Cole*) in subsequent years, including the horrific attacks of September 11, 2001.

Today we have better perspective regarding bin Laden's impact on the world, including energy and security. Around the globe we're fighting militants inspired by his views, and we can see with each passing day how far and deep his reach goes. We are engaged in war against him and his forces in the Middle East. Some of our closest allies, including the British, have suffered direct Al Qaeda attacks as well as uncovered Al Qaeda plots against their own security. Further, Saudi Arabia recently announced the discovery of extensive plans by bin Laden's organization to bomb and disable oil facilities in that country. In April 2007, more than 170 suspected participants in these plots were arrested in Saudi Arabia.

Bin Laden makes a point of targeting such critical oil infrastructure because he knows what a devastating impact he can have on the world's economy, even on the fundamentals of the global market system, by attacking oil. That's a part of his strategy that many Americans haven't been properly alerted to. It's terrorism—energy and oil terrorism.

He knows that the United States is dependent on foreign oil, that our economy remains more oil-intensive than that of other developed nations, and that we suffer more than most other countries when oil prices rise. That alone gives bin Laden a special interest in attacking oil infrastructure. Taking the long view, bin Laden believes that the United States is vulnerable to volatility in oil prices while lacking the discipline and vision to wean itself off oil. Oil is an attractive way for bin Laden and others to attack the United States in a fundamentally long-term and economically damaging fashion.

Attacking oil facilities and pipelines has become common in Iraq, and the strategy is spreading across the globe. Google "terrorist pipeline attack" and you'll see an alarmingly large number of hits, growing all the time.

Bin Laden sees the United States as a sleeping giant—one that he wrongly believes will never wake up. He believes that we will stick to our old energy policies and technologies because we have lost our vision and our focus. Like others around the world who consider the United States to be a profligate energy user, he thinks we can't change.

We don't know for certain how much of our oil spending

goes to terrorist organizations. But we do know that bin Laden, whose fortune derives from his Saudi construction family, would never have been a significant influence on world affairs without the oil profit and revenue that flowed into the world's largest oil nation. And we know that certain oil-rich nations—including Libya, Iran, Iraq, and Sudan—have used their oil wealth to support terrorism around the world.

This problem has greatly intensified since 1997. The price increase in world oil markets since 2004 alone, when prices were already much higher than in the late 1990s, has resulted in the largest-ever transfers of wealth from oil-consumer nations to oil-producer nations. A recent report by economists from the Federal Reserve Bank of New York says that oil exporters received about $1 trillion for their oil in 2006—about three times what they received in 2002.

There's an additional threat to our national security and our position as the world's economic powerhouse. We are feeding a huge trade deficit, attracting few of those petrodollars back to the United States in the form of purchases that support our economy and borrowing significant amounts in international markets to support our national debt. While these are all bad enough in the short term, they threaten our economic security and position over the long term. With our addiction to oil, we are weakening our economic security as well as our national security. Do our trade deficit and dependence on foreign oil help explain today's very weak dollar? Without a doubt they play a large role.

In 1997 the Taliban could harbor an international criminal like bin Laden despite Western threats because its deeply impoverished nation had literally nothing to lose—but Saddam Hussein was in the international community's crosshairs. In November

1997, after months of wrangling between Saddam and the UN weapons inspectors, my diplomatic team and I worked closely with the members of the UN Security Council to pass a unanimous resolution condemning Iraq for defying weapons inspectors. The council also imposed a foreign travel ban on top Iraqi officials. While there were disagreements among members, we worked until every member of the council—including France, Russia, and China—voted for the resolution.

Members of the Bush administration act as if just projecting and using military force, as they did in removing Saddam from power, is the way to solve the world's problems. Yet our experience in 1997, working multilaterally to control and contain Saddam, brought us together with other powerful nations. Alongside inspections and sanctions against Saddam, we employed military force in a concerted and strategic way in collaboration with our allies, patrolling Iraq's skies and the Persian Gulf and preventing any action by Saddam. We were united with our allies, even though it required a lot of work. Today, having used military force almost unilaterally to invade Iraq and depose Saddam, and having conducted the Iraq war and reconstruction so badly, we are isolated. Further, we have let regional extremism and ethnic/religious hatred out of containment. As a result, Iraq is in civil war, and it is a territory upon which different regional influences can fight out their differences.

In 1997 the whole Security Council of the United Nations sent a very clear message to Iraq: back off. You have to restore UNSCOM (the UN inspection team) and you have to start behaving. There are going to be consequences unless you do. Although Saddam flouted some of the UN requirements, we know now that the pressure was enough to keep him from restarting his nuclear program. Further, with Western aircraft patrolling the no-fly zone, we knew he was contained and no threat to his

31

neighbors, as he had been prior to the first Gulf War. International cooperation and discipline worked better than scare tactics and unilateral action.

In 1997 the Kyoto Protocol was finalized and went out for adoption. Kyoto was the outgrowth of a series of international meetings and research projects aimed at atmospheric pollution, which was then thought to be involved in long-term warming of the global climate. In response, the U.S. Senate adopted a non-binding resolution saying it would reject the Kyoto agreement if it would create significant damage to the U.S. economy. (This resolution, by the way, is sometimes mischaracterized as a flat rejection of the Kyoto treaty by the United States.) The Senate was more concerned about protecting the economy than about protecting the atmosphere, partly because in those days it seemed as if we had to choose one or the other and partly because we didn't yet know how much it would cost not to act.

Today we know better. Panels of international scientists have made it clear that we need to reduce emissions trends very soon if we wish to prevent changes in the atmosphere that would produce damaging and irreversible impacts on Earth's surface, affecting people, ecosystems, the world economy, weather patterns, and more. In 1997 that kind of thinking and evidence hadn't come to dominate our science and policy. There was a lot of skepticism about the science of global warming and climate change. The general feeling among developed nations was that this might be a concern, but it certainly wasn't obvious that everyone needed to leap into action. For instance, only in 1997, with Prime Minister Tony Blair's ascent to office in Britain, did that nation start leading the charge on global climate policy.

Here in the United States, even though Vice President Al

Gore had drawn attention to climate change in *Earth in the Balance*, a book published in 1992 before he became vice president, the Clinton administration and Congress were not mobilized to take climate policy action. The vice president signed on to Kyoto for the United States in 1998, an action President George W. Bush personally and vocally reversed very early in his presidency. So, as a nation, we have gone hot and cold on climate policy over the past ten years.

What a difference a decade makes. In 2007 the Intergovernmental Panel on Climate Change has released several major research studies, conducted and reviewed by thousands of the world's leading scientists, saying that climate change *is* occurring, that humans *are* the likely cause, and that emissions trends *must* be reversed within about a decade or we face disastrous impacts around the world. Further, there is widespread acceptance that the costs of acting to prevent climate change are far less than the risk and potential cost of *not* acting to prevent climate change.

In 1997, as UN ambassador, I was one of the American policymakers most visible to the rest of the world. I spoke with ambassadors from small island nations who were deeply concerned about the risk of rising sea levels and how their countries might literally disappear under the waves. I spoke with ambassadors from undeveloped countries where desertification had already taken a huge toll on agriculture and food supplies, with prospects for far worse impacts as global warming intensified. I guess you could say that even though I was living in the ambassador's residence on the forty-second floor of the Waldorf Astoria in New York City, I was on the front lines of the international global warming debate. Some is scientific; much is human.

I particularly remember the deep concern expressed to me by the representative of the Cape Verde Islands. His small nation, at sea level and not a world power, had no ability to address climate change or sea-level rise on its own. As he told me, his nation needed larger nations that consume large amounts of fossil energy to change their habits before polar ice melts and raises sea levels. He sought me out because he thought the United States could help lead this kind of national and international effort. He was right. We can.

Unlike some climate change skeptics, I didn't see an anti-American motivation behind the climate change dialogue, as purported by those in the United States who thought it was simply an effort to slow down the American economy and force economic development to other parts of the world.

Why not? First, the agreement called for sharper emissions reductions in European countries than in the United States. Even though our economy is more energy-intensive than Europe's, we were not singled out for the most severe reductions. The Kyoto treaty recognized that we are a larger nation and more spread out than some, and that reducing our emissions might be a larger task. Second, I saw real distress and concern among undeveloped nations, who somewhat fairly believed that the United States had built its vast economic strength on a foundation of burning carbon-heavy fossil fuels such as coal and oil. They were worried that we would continue our energy consumption patterns while other nations would be forced to stay in poverty, or even disappear in the rising sea.

It is fossil carbon—released from Earth's crust when we dig up and burn coal or oil or natural gas—that constitutes the largest global warming threat. Burning wood or other biologically derived carbon (such as biofuels) is less of an issue, because it doesn't add to the net balance of carbon in the atmosphere and on Earth's surface; the carbon cycles around, roughly, among plants and organisms and the oceans and atmosphere.

This distinction between atmospheric carbon cycling via renewable fuels and releasing fossil carbon into the atmosphere is one of the most confusing issues in the climate debate.

When coal consumption increased rapidly with the growth of Western economies in the 1800s, it displaced wood-fired systems for transportation and heating—systems that recycle carbon already in the atmosphere. Coal brought geologic carbon to the surface and added it to atmospheric carbon. Then oil consumption rose rapidly (at a rate of more than 4 percent annually in post–World War II America), adding even more fossil carbon into the atmosphere.

Fossil carbon from oil and coal, and to a lesser degree natural gas, explains rising atmospheric carbon dioxide concentrations, which increase the atmosphere's ability to retain heat.

Deconstructing the past decade, as we have been doing, we see one marked measurement that seems to prove that global warming is occurring. Over those ten years, several were among the dozen or so warmest years on record. Our temperature records go back reliably only a couple of centuries, so that statistic may not be as shocking as some others showing that atmospheric carbon dioxide has never been higher in the past 600,000 years. Analysis of global temperature indicators such as ice fields and forests show that the globe is at a hot point and getting hotter, even measured over millions of years.

I think former Vice President Al Gore's more recent book and documentary, *An Inconvenient Truth*, does an excellent job of laying out the scientific basis for the concern that global warming is happening, is accelerating, and is closely related to our combustion of fossil fuels.

I saw the former vice president give his global warming presentation at an international mayors' meeting in Utah in 2005. This was the PowerPoint presentation that became the basis of his documentary film that received Academy Award recognition and might, a month or two after publication of this book, bring the former vice president a Nobel Peace Prize.

While there, I saw Robert Redford, a longtime conservationist and friend who sponsored the mayors' event at his Sundance resort and had asked me to come and give a speech. (In 2001 and 2002, Redford and I served together on the board of directors of the Natural Resources Defense Council, or NRDC. That organization has been concerned about global warming for years, so as a board member I learned more about the climate issue, as well as ways to address it.) I met local leaders from around America and around the world, an inspiring group of people mobilized for energy and climate action.

Seeing the vice president's presentation, I couldn't help but notice the sharp difference between the personality, the vision, and the policy sense of our vice presidents in 1997 and today.

Gore and Vice President Dick Cheney have diverse interests and strong opinions, and each has a head full of knowledge about almost everything. In fact, Cheney is pretty darned sure he does know everything. He lives the luxurious life of someone who has nothing left to learn. And he's figured out how to sound conservative while projecting the most radical and dangerous energy policies presented by anyone in the White House in the past fifty years or more. He's a conservative who doesn't believe in conservation.

Cheney proclaimed in the early part of the George W. Bush administration that conservation, though a "personal virtue," hardly constitutes the basis of a sound energy policy. (He's wrong, by the way. Efficiency and conservation are the first, most cost-effective, and fastest ways to meet energy demand. I will address that later, particularly in chapter 6.) In contrast, Vice President Gore is a strong and knowledgeable proponent of diversifying our energy supplies while reducing our emissions.

Vice President Cheney oversaw the preparation of the most shortsighted energy policy anyone could ever imagine. It was apparently his top priority coming into office, and he was determined to get it adopted. After only a couple of months as vice president, he convened a group of energy industry people (his office will not reveal who participated) and stuck together a wish list that would sharply increase our nation's addiction to oil.

Cheney's 2001 National Energy Policy was replete with misconceived prescriptions: drill, drill, drill across the United States, in the Arctic, on the Outer Continental Shelf, in the Rockies; speed up permitting processes and make oil and gas development the prescribed priority use on public lands; increase refining capacity at the expense of local permitting concerns; and so on.

Have you ever known someone whose father made him smoke a whole cigar when he was young—throat burning, eyes watering, lungs convulsing, maybe throwing up—just to kill his interest in smoking? I can only hope that's what Vice President Cheney thought he was doing for America. But I doubt it.

At that Sundance meeting I spent some private time with Vice President Gore talking policy and politics, as well as the specifics of his case on climate change. We had a nice lunch in one of Redford's villas.

When a security agent drove us back down to the amphitheater where Gore would make his presentation after lunch, I sat in the front seat, with Gore right behind me on the passenger side. We pulled up at the semicircle at the theater, and one of my staff people opened the car's front and back doors simultaneously, asking, "How do you guys decide who gets the front seat?"

Without missing a beat, Gore almost shouted, pointing at me. "He just *took* it!"

He was kidding around. But it does point out something about us. He may have been right long before the rest of us, but when I get my chance to make a difference, I take a back seat to no one.

At the Sundance mayors' summit, I was impressed with Redford's commitment on the issue of global warming, not just the former vice president's. Addressing the mayors, he spoke earnestly, quietly, from the heart. He talked about personal issues, not just big policy concerns: How will our energy consumption affect the billions of poor people around the world who will feel the effects of climate change most severely? What kind of world are we going to leave for future generations? Are we willing to risk their future for our own shortsighted consumption? Redford also commended the mayors, who sit closer to the people than do federal and state officials. It's hard for them to act independently of federal policy without federal incentives, but they are trying, and getting a lot done. Redford rightly recognized their pervasive and influential policy role.

The mayors' climate change coalition, led by Seattle mayor Greg Nickles, is an interesting response to climate change. Again, it shows a difference between 1997 and 2007. In 1997, we thought the only way to address climate change was with a strong federal and international policy. Today, we have made at least some progress with the vigorous response of cities, states, and regions. This is not to say that the national and international policies are unnecessary—they are critical. But action can start at the most local level, and we can hope that it will then push the federal government to do the right thing.

What can cities do? Since 1997, many city governments have decided to buy more hybrid and flex-fuel cars. They are planning parks and open spaces to reduce the "heat island" effect of large urban masses of buildings, streets, and parking lots. They are encouraging the use of public transit and bike trails and designing "transit-oriented development" to make it convenient and enjoyable for people to drive less. The states are doing big things as well. They are implementing new green building codes and public building requirements that could reduce energy use by 50 percent. They are requiring utilities to provide higher percentages of renewable power—something my New Mexico colleague Senator Jeff Bingaman has tried repeatedly to get Congress to agree to, so far without success. They are eliminating the sales tax on hybrid automobiles. They are enacting policies to sharply reduce greenhouse gas emissions in their states and in both multi-state and single-state programs. The Western Climate Initiative that I started up with California, Oregon, Washington, and Arizona (and now including Utah) is an example of a regional effort to reduce climate-changing emissions across a number of states, so that we don't simply move emissions from our own state and see them appear in another.

Climate change policy must be international, too, and unfortunately the United States has taken large backward steps in that regard since 1997. But here in 2007, despite the failure of the Bush administration and Congress to adopt good, strong energy and climate policy, and despite the fact that we have lost—given away, abdicated—our leadership role in the world in many respects, the American people are ready to change. They see the importance; they see the benefits; they approve of what their states and cities are doing. The polls show strong support for national and international efforts, even if they cost a significant amount, to address the problems.

Companies are changing, too. Not every company, but business in general is embracing energy efficiency and energy alternatives. Investment capital is flowing into new energy alternatives at an unprecedented rate, partly as a function of higher energy prices but also because some investors are truly visionary and committed to a new energy future.

Look at Bill Ford, who pushed for greener cars over the past decade. Look at how BP is investing in new carbon-removal technologies as well as alternative fuels. Watch billionaire Vinod Khosla, a founder of Sun Microsystems and a key Silicon Valley investor, as he explores and invests in more than forty new alternative energy ventures. See how airplane manufacturers are reducing fuel demand. Observe how the investment group taking over Texas's largest utility, TXU—a group including former EPA administrator Bill Reilly—committed publicly to dropping proposals for eight conventional coal plants and sharply increasing investment in energy efficiency, under pressure from national and local environmental groups, mayors, and citizens.

Sir Richard Branson, who is helping us get a spaceport started in New Mexico, wants to use renewable fuels for his jets and spacecraft. He's very enthusiastic about this stuff—a wealthy and successful entrepreneur and visionary who puts his money into sensible, moneymaking alternatives. In my home state, beside Branson, we have wind developers, solar-cell builders, and electric-car manufacturers. People are getting large state tax credits to install solar electric panels and solar hot water, and they don't have to pay sales tax when they buy a hybrid automobile. Ten years ago we did not have even a small fraction of the interest and investment we have seen recently in our new clean-energy economy.

The change in business and popular attitudes alone is a huge and wonderful difference between 1997 and 2007. It makes all the other, more negative differences between 1997 and today— our failure to embrace hybrid technology, the challenge represented by Osama bin Laden, the climate-changing contrast between Dick Cheney and Al Gore as vice presidents—look small. The private sector, from investors to manufacturers to consumers, is starting to head in the right direction (mostly). We have reason to be optimistic, not only because we can see the error of our ways since 1997, but also because people are seeing the need for change and joining the call for action. They are ready for leadership on challenging issues—leadership like that showcased by FDR and JFK when the nation was challenged in other ways. The people are ready for bold moves, bold policy, instead of purported policy that avoids real change. The year 2007 marks the beginning of a very new, very different decade.

The ten years from 1997 to 2007 featured no major supply disruption. There was no war to protect Saudi Arabia or to remove Iraq from Kuwait, as there had been in 1991. There was no oil embargo, as occurred twice in the 1970s. There was, in short, no dramatic single event that signaled the failure of U.S. energy policy. But the problems have been building in the veins of our economy like so much petroleum plaque, and we all know that economic heart disease could be the result. There is no better word for the way we've fallen short on energy, security, and climate policy than "dangerous."

However, in the face of this danger, I am upbeat because I know we're ready to turn a corner. We know we got stuck in a dark alley. We know we need to go in a new direction. Compared to 1997, 2007 marks the beginning of a new national consensus and a new commitment to doing what's in our own best long-term interests.

CHAPTER 3

Oil, Coal, and the Planet's Future

The world's oil is largely controlled by nationalized oil companies and the great oil cartel, OPEC (the Organization of the Petroleum Exporting Countries). It's not a free, competitive world market. Worse, some of the dollars we spend on foreign oil are passed through to terrorists and organizations—even nations—hostile to the United States and the West. This results in direct attacks against us and our allies. It makes the world unsafe. It threatens economic investment and markets.

Oil dependence is an insidious threat, not as obvious as the ones that JFK and FDR stood up to with the national will behind them. We use the gas pumps every day, but we don't really know where each gallon comes from. The companies that deliver oil have perfected a highly efficient global system of finding, developing, transporting, refining, and retailing it. Few of us are aware of growing foreign oil dependence, the amount of money we transfer to other nations as petrodollars, or trends in Asian and U.S. consumption that are radically changing the world oil market. Nor are we aware of the deals international oil companies make to secure access to the oil managed by national oil companies across the globe.

Morally speaking, oil undermines America's leadership role in the world. Our addiction to oil turns us from a freedom-loving, idealistic Dr. Jekyll into an oil-seeking, greedy Mr. Hyde. This sounds dramatic, but the world sees the inconsistency when the United States preaches freedom and human rights, and then purchases oil from or protects tyrannical dictatorships. The world sees that our foreign policy becomes oriented to scanning or scouring the world for oil and protecting oil where it lies, rather than protecting our real national security interests and fairness, freedom, and civil government within and among nations.

The two greatest acronymic presidents, FDR and JFK, led the nation to meet important challenges. Admittedly, both were short-term challenges that were more visible and whose solutions were very clear. But the energy challenge facing us today is a great—even day-to-day—threat. If we don't deal with it, we doom ourselves to being held hostage by other nations or individuals who control or threaten oil supplies. I will discuss this further, with the example of Iran's seizure of fifteen British sailors and soldiers in March 2007, in chapter 4.

FDR and JFK led the nation to take on significant, important challenges—and to deal with them with crisp dispatch. We have not done the same thing in energy policy. We enacted fuel efficiency standards in the 1970s after the first OPEC oil embargo, but when the price of oil stabilized, toward the mid-1980s, without the prospect of a new oil embargo, we let those standards stagnate. At that point, oil producers, not oil consumers, were on the ropes. Oil was relatively cheap.

46

America didn't keep pushing for energy independence because we didn't think it was necessary anymore, owing to immediate market conditions. I think most people, in the back of their minds, probably would have agreed that we weren't taking the long view. But very few pushed for long-term energy policy under those conditions. We just can't afford to keep making energy policy that way. We need to take the reins, apply the spurs, and ride hard. This is no time for cantering, sauntering through a twenty-year fog of different ideas and approaches.

My overarching goals are a 50 percent reduction in petroleum use by 2020 and an 80 percent reduction in global warming emissions by 2040.

Think about that. I'm saying that we, as Americans, can cut the amount of oil we use in half in just a little over a decade. It will require national determination and the will to change. It won't be easy, but like the other great challenges we have faced as a nation, the dramatic reduction in oil demand must be achieved, and quickly.

We can do it if we all feel it's essential for the future of our nation. We can't do it if each American keeps hoping someone else will solve the problem for the rest of us. We can fashion our own future so that it is dependent on what you and I do or on what some oil-possessing dictator or cartel decides for us. I know which side I'm choosing.

For decades politicians protected the American people from a gasoline tax proposed by some as a means to fund alternatives that would have created energy price competition and alternatives. I don't support a heavy-handed gas tax because it would put the burden mostly on the backs of the everyday people who keep our country running. It wouldn't be fair and it could lead to serious economic problems for households and small businesses and farms all the way to the gross national product and our rate of economic growth. I think there are better ways to solve the energy and climate problem than across-the-board taxes (see pages 144–145). Yet what has happened without the gasoline tax hasn't been fair, either. Instead of paying a gasoline tax or bringing alternatives to market in a more practical way, Americans have had to pay far more to the oil companies, with demonstrably negative progress in reducing our oil dependence.

Dependence on oil is the direct result of the nation's failure to get on a sensible, sustainable energy pathway. We don't have plug-in cars or significant alternative fuels. We don't have safe, effective, affordable transportation options within most of our metro areas or between cities.

The nation that put people on the moon, that helped bring two world wars to decisive and victorious ends, and that has exported the concepts of freedom and democracy around the world is not a nation that should find itself servant to the master of international oil.

What I will do is what many others have promised. I will break our dependence on oil. It will require technological ingenuity, some sensible policy changes, and a determination to think longer-term and not to be greedy. We're all going to have to make changes. Some might call it sacrifice: some might call it investment. Making progress will cost everybody something— and save everyone far more. We shouldn't ask the working public to shoulder the burden—it's up to everyone to help out, from the corporate boardroom to the refinery to the halls of academia.

This is not a campaign to turn down thermostats, put on sweaters, or ration gasoline. It isn't about cardigan sweaters or cold fingers and toes. We have learned a lot since the 1970s. We know that we can easily achieve a 100-mile-per-gallon car—at least economically and technologically—without sacrificing safety or speed. We know that modern technologies allow us to collect and store wind and solar power so that they become our major source of electrical power. Further, we know that our plentiful natural gas and coal supplies can be used far more efficiently and with much less impact on our climate.

Some of these steps may seem expensive. Compared to the cost of importing oil, however, they are very affordable. Compared to the increased cost of natural gas alone, they will save us hundreds of billions of dollars. Compared to the costs of letting other nations become the world's technological leaders, my proposals are eminently cost-effective. Compared to the costs of having to plan our national security around the whims of any despot sitting on black gold, this approach is practically free. The truth is, if you see the world for what it is, change won't be expensive at all. And when you consider the global climate calamity scientists are warning about, you have to ask: Is there really even a choice?

The underlying problem is that our elected officials—from the president through Congress and right into the state legislatures and governors' offices—have been afraid to ask the American people to pay these relatively small costs, instead allowing the country to drive itself into an energy and climate ditch. Most of us pay for health insurance or life insurance, and it's time for this nation to pay for some energy insurance. In the long run, we'll save a lot of money and avoid a lot of pain.

The real cost, though, will be felt by the politicians who rely on money from oil companies and coal producers to get elected. I have taken plenty of funding from these sources in the past, and I have always told them, "I will hear you out, but don't expect me to do what you say." (As a result, I am not always their favorite guy.)

These companies will profit if they participate and adapt, but they can't cling to the old business models. Regardless of their reactions, we will need tough decisions even if they are opposed by the auto industry or the companies that move oil around the world or that build conventional coal plants.

I know that some in the energy industry will say that my proposals can't be done, that continued dependence on oil (and necessarily on foreign oil) is inevitable, even desirable. They call it "energy interdependence" and say it's good for the world. To a small degree this may be true. But I want to propose a much different, achievable pathway to energy security—not energy interdependence—for the United States. That is what America needs.

As a former diplomat, I ask: Why are we alone in the world today?

We are alone in the world at least in part because our leaders have abdicated their responsibility to create and implement energy policy. Instead of deciding that the United States should create the incentives for new technologies and diverse domestic energy sources, we have been distracted and have avoided the short-term costs that reap long-term benefits. We have failed to protect our national interests.

The international oil companies are now a superpower, just as nations once were. We can't depend on them to bail us out. These corporations have been doing their job, and very well. It isn't their job to take care of the United States. It isn't their job to find and develop alternative energy sources or to spread freedom and democracy. It isn't their job to defend our nation's oil interests overseas, or the shipping lanes such as the Persian Gulf, which are so critical to both the world trade in petroleum and the stability of oil prices and the world economy.

Their job is to make a profit and pass it on to shareholders. That is the beauty of our economic system. It's a model that has built progress and prosperity across the globe, raising the standard of living and fulfilling the hopes and dreams of billions, including the fortunate and hard-working residents of the United States.

But that model cannot protect U.S. national interests, either at home or abroad. Congress, the states, and the president have responsibility for that.

It's a critical responsibility that they haven't lived up to.

Since 2001, despite the fact that oil prices are bleeding us dry, Congress and the president have really been sitting on their hands, watching the game. The ballyhooed Energy Policy Act of 2005 was a thick stack of Band-Aids, not a bold new cure for a nation whose reliance on foreign oil was creeping ever upward and whose energy consumption and contributions to global warming were the talk of the world. In fact, in my view, the Energy Policy Act of 2005 was far too strongly influenced by the large players in the energy industry—particularly the oil and gas companies that are so close to the White House and to the fossil-friendly leaders of the Republican Party who then controlled Congress.

Those same players have generally spent the last six years denying the threat of global warming and then claiming that their weak policies and more research would effectively combat it. They have claimed that addressing global warming in a meaningful way would hurt the American economy, a position that I strongly dispute because it is clear that our economy will suffer far worse damage if we fail to stop global warming in concert with other nations.

In fact, the American people have been paying such huge price premiums for oil and natural gas in the past few years that we have found ourselves supporting the oil companies' profits instead of our own energy diversification. A small fraction of those overpayments, if spent on new energy programs and incentives to diversify into alternative technologies and fuels, would have set our nation on an entirely different pathway.

In a recent high-budget advertising campaign, the oil giant Chevron has made the claim that energy independence is unattainable; instead the world should embrace a concept that Chevron calls "energy interdependence." Chevron says that no nation in the world is energy-independent (which is most certainly true). I agree that total energy independence is not achievable, and in the following pages I use the term loosely to indicate a situation in which we are no more than 10 to 20 percent dependent on foreign oil, mostly from our neighbors in Mexico and Canada, who provide about that percentage of our oil today. Quoting from Chevron's print advertisement (which I saw in the March 3, 2007, edition of *The Economist* and which has reprinted everywhere from *Foreign Affairs* magazine to the *New York Times*), "The fact is that the vast majority of countries rely on the few energy-producing nations that won the geological lottery." True again, hopelessly and regrettably true—and reason enough to get off oil.

Chevron's pitch is that we should build a cooperative world energy system. "True global energy security will be a result of cooperation and engagement, not isolationism. When investment and expertise are allowed to flow freely across borders, the engine of innovation is ignited, prosperity is fueled, and the energy available to everyone increases."

But Chevron's view that we should support "energy interdependence" is fatally wrong. For a hundred years we have put our trust in the oil companies to deliver the energy America needs, particularly in recent decades when oil imports have again crept up to around 65 percent of our total oil demand. Our energy interdependence has created a dependence we can't afford.

Imports create vulnerability. Imports allow other nations to hold us hostage. The world oil development and transportation system doesn't defend itself—the United States spends more than $100 billion every year to defend the Persian Gulf and other oil hot spots around the globe.

Worst of all, however, oil imports make us into a very different nation. Since we can't live without all that oil, we coddle kings and dictators, we defend our interest in oil more than our interest in democracy, and we subsidize the international oil trade with the lives of our sailors and soldiers. Instead of being the world's beacon of freedom and prosperity, we are suspected of invading Iraq under a false casus belli that hid a larger interest in the world's second-richest oilfields.

Another reason Chevron's argument for energy interdependence is wrong is that the prospects for the peaceful resolution of the conflicts surrounding the world's richest oil regions, particularly the Persian Gulf, are so dim at this moment. It will take years, maybe decades or centuries, to resolve some of these problems. The concept of general peace and cooperation among nations and peoples who have been enemies for centuries, even millennia, may be a chimera. Concerned nations might get them to agree on strategies that prevent outright war, but they aren't going to be "peaceful" anytime soon.

The oil companies, and unfortunately the United States at this moment, have virtually no credibility when they call for cooperation and engagement, for peaceful resolution of differences so that energy and investment may freely flow. The Bush administration, with the support of its compliant GOP Congress, has wasted the credibility this nation once commanded and deserved. It has failed to create the energy diversity, technology, and alternatives that will reduce our almost singular dependence on petroleum for liquid transportation fuel.

I do agree, strongly, with two points made in the Chevron advertisement.

First, I agree with Chevron's statement that "once we all start to think differently about energy, then we can truly make this promise a reality."

This is true, especially if you read it closely. Chevron says we need to think differently about *energy*, not just about oil. If these oil superpowers were truly committed to energy production (not just oil production), we could quickly create the diversity of energy sources that will fuel a healthy global economy and create competitive national and international energy markets. But I have also heard from oil companies for years that it is unrealistic to expect any other energy source to displace oil in the next thirty or fifty years. In fact, at a Western Governors' Association meeting two years ago, Shell Oil's U.S. leader said that oil will still be 95 percent or more dominant in thirty years. If it is, our country is doomed. We need to break this addiction, not accept it.

Oil is energy, but all energy isn't oil. The oil superpowers have successfully built a smooth-running international oil trading system, one that has fueled a hundred years of growth and prosperity—but one that is dangerously dependent on the winners of what Chevron calls the "geologic lottery." The richest oil region

54

in the world, around the Persian Gulf, is perhaps also the most unstable region in the world.

First question: Wouldn't it be great if these countries could play nicely and send us their oil?

Second question: Is that the basis of a real energy policy that protects America's interests?

It's ridiculous to pin this nation's, or the world's, future on a collaborative relationship among oil-producing and oil-consuming nations. Among the world's top ten oil-producing nations, there are few that we could call stable, and several that are overtly hostile to the United States.

Most of these are not nations we can count on. Yet we are addicted to what they produce, and the multinational oil companies are not in the market to help us develop alternatives that will support market competition and energy diversity.

The second part of Chevron's advertisement that I agree with is that successful energy policy doesn't have to come at anyone's expense. But once again, I read that statement very differently from the way Chevron intended us to.

Truly successful energy policy will save consumers money and strengthen America's economy. When we work with our allies to implement these policies around the world, almost every country will find sustainable energy resources within or near its borders and every nation will have access to affordable energy-efficient technologies that will displace the ones so dependent on oil today.

I trust that I am not giving the impression that I am singling out Chevron. That's not what I am doing. Chevron undertook a noble but misguided high-budget advertising campaign, and I am merely offering it as an example of where our nation's interests and those of a dominant oil superpower diverge. And I am saying that we can't put our trust in these players, or their political allies in Congress and the White House, to do what needs to be done in the national interest.

I think our leaders should meet with these people, consider their ideas and suggestions and perspectives, just as they should with other interests. But what our leaders have done instead is to follow the oil companies' lead. That, by definition, isn't leading, it's following. What the United States needs right now is leadership. We have been badly served on energy and climate policy. Our leaders have dug us deeper into an already deep hole.

I mentioned earlier that my state, New Mexico, is an energy-producing state. Many people don't realize that we produce the second-highest quantity of onshore natural gas, and the fourth- or fifth-highest amount of oil among the states, depending on the year. We share the huge and prolific (and declining) Permian Basin with Texas, where many millionaires were made in the oil business just as they were in New Mexico, and with Mexico. Thus, New Mexico is an oil and gas state. We also export large amounts of electricity produced mostly at coal plants in the Four Corners area, although a wind company recently concluded our first wind energy export deal and is exporting New Mexico wind energy to Arizona customers. (At the last minute, when an unexpected right-of-way issue threatened to prevent final financing of this wind-export project, I worked through the night with our utilities and the state's largest private landowner to make sure it could proceed smoothly. I credit that landowner, who probably would prefer to remain nameless, for his singular cooperation on a very tight timeline, as well as his commitment to renewable energy development in New Mexico.)

So I am very familiar with the oil industry. I know how to work with them, and I know how to say no in ways that Congress and the president apparently never learned. The industry's leaders haven't been pleased with many of my energy and climate policies for New Mexico. As I say, I am not their favorite politician. But I know that the public interest, both in New Mexico and nationally, requires elected officials to take some responsibility, not just get comfortable with the interests who have the most power and want the most return on their political investment.

As I said, oil is energy, but all energy is not oil.

As governor of a leading energy state, in a few short years I have enacted some of the most aggressive renewable energy and energy efficiency programs in the country. I have successfully pushed our state, with its tremendous amount of oil and gas, to think beyond oil and gas.

I have tried very hard, and with a significant measure of success, to diversify our state's energy economy. That's what our country needs to do. Other people (including presidential candidates) talk about it, but I have actually done it.

I haven't focused just on my state, either. Being a former cabinet member, a former congressman, and a former United Nations ambassador, I have used my influence to advocate for similar strategies across the West.

I jumped at the chance to become chairman of the Western Governors' Association in my second year as governor because I saw the potential to change the region's course and direction.

The West has long been a place where the energy industries have held the upper hand. You could call it the Oil and Coal Corral. Much of our economic progress and economic development have come from the energy and mineral industries—from digging up, moving, and selling what was underground. But there are other important industries here as well, such as ranching and tourism, and there are communities that want to preserve hunting and fishing for the future. They don't want to sell their birthright for a mess of pottage, as the biblical saying goes. They want balance; they want protection of basic needs and interests. They don't want to dig everything up and sell it right now.

I have been excited to see how some of that fundamentally conservative philosophy has come back to the surface in the West in recent years in the face of the Bush administration's no-holds-barred assault on Western public lands and resources. And I think the fact that Westerners have called for more balance, including alternative energy policies that bring renewable energy into the marketplace in a significant way, is more support for my belief that America has the right stuff to reclaim its place in the world by adopting balanced energy and climate policies both at home and abroad.

In other words, with policy and leadership like what we have had across the West in recent years, the United States does not need to be, and will not be, alone in the world for very long.

Let me give you an example of the new Western leadership.

In 2004, California governor Arnold Schwarzenegger and I successfully proposed some new energy goals for the eighteen states that were then members of the Western Governors' Association. "Arnold," as everyone on Earth knows him, had just been elected governor and agreed with me during a phone conversation that we should work together to change the direction of energy policy in the Western states, where so much of America's energy is produced. Mostly, it's from traditional fossil energy sources such as coal, oil, and natural gas. But the region has enormous renewable energy potential in the form of wind, geothermal, and solar energy. And because energy has been relatively cheap in the West, it also has great potential for energy efficiency.

After our phone call, I flew out to California in January 2004 to see Arnold as he was preparing to take office. We met in his Santa Monica film production office, an impressive room that showcases his achievements in the entertainment business. Surrounded by awards and artifacts from his career in film, we talked about energy policy and climate change and the significant influence that California could have on how the West produces and uses energy.

I have seen some of the impacts of being an energy hinterland, or breadbasket, or colony, for the rest of the United States. Thus, when I went out to see Governor Schwarzenegger, whose state consumes far more energy than it produces, I went as governor of an energy-producing, energy-exporting state.

Our conversation started with his recollection that we had met once before, when I attended a campaign event for presidential candidate Al Gore at Schwarzenegger's home in 2000. Of course, Arnold has Democratic tendencies, but the host of the event was his wife, Maria Shriver, a member of the longtime Democratic Kennedy clan. Arnold, a Republican, had greeted the people coming to his home and graciously disappeared so as neither to endanger his own GOP connections nor to eavesdrop on the Democratic strategy to capture the White House.

Reminiscing with Arnold four years later about that Democratic fund-raising event at his home, I was glad to remember that he had not stayed to circulate with us Democrats, because Senator Ted Kennedy and I eventually got up and started singing to the group. I didn't want Arnold to have that image of me as we sat down to discuss the future of energy in the West.

Arnold greeted me and immediately said, in his thick Austrian accent, "I met you at the Gore fund-raiser at my house in 2000." I nodded, not knowing what was coming next. "You and

Teddy Kennedy got up and started singing. It was horrible," asserted the Terminator, with an emphasis on the word "horrible." I had used the same word to describe the Kennedy/Richardson duet when I told my staff about it on the way to California the day before.

Taken aback despite my years of negotiating with terrorists and dictators (not to compare them with Governor Schwarzenegger), I said, "Governor, I had no idea you heard that. I agree it was horrible, but I thought you had left the event."

"No," said Arnold, arriving at his punch line, again delivered with that strong accent. "I did hear that horrible singing. I was only out in the kitchen—cleaning up after the Democrats, just like I am doing now!"

The story has a partisan edge, unfortunately. As far as energy issues, it wasn't the Democrats who screwed up the California situation—in fact, we came to the rescue when Enron, a GOP-oriented company that supported President Bush's election and later went into an economy-shaking bankruptcy full of criminal proceedings, gamed and destroyed the energy distribution system in California in the late 1990s. Treasury Secretary Larry Summers, then governor Gray Davis, and I spent weeks and months focused on keeping California out of electrical trouble.

That may explain why Enron energy traders were taped making coarse remarks about me in my last days as energy secretary in 2000. Those tapes came to light a few years later and showed how the Enron people really felt about the Clinton administration. I am proud to have been the energy secretary Enron loved to hate. Because of my energetic pursuit of the facts in the Enron situation, according to transcripts made by the Snohomish, Washington, Public Utility District, Enron traders called me "that [bleepin'] Richardson." On June 9, 2004, working from those transcripts, a reporter for the *Seattle Post-Intelligencer* wrote: "The boys at Enron couldn't wait for Clinton to leave, along with his secretary of energy. 'That [bleepin'] Bill Richardson,' said one energy trader. 'He's [bleepin'] gone!' exulted another. The traders rejoiced at the role their parent company and its chairman, Ken Lay—'Kenny Boy' as he was nicknamed by President George W. Bush—played in backing the eventual winner of the 2000 campaign. 'You know who the biggest contributor is to Bush?,' said one trader. The voice on the other end wonders if anybody gave more money, or loaned out the corporate jet more often, than the big 'E.' 'Ken Lay is going to be the next secretary of energy,' the first voice jokes. 'That would be awesome,' says the voice on the other end of the line."

Sorry, traders, I'm ba-aack! And where is Enron these days, having bankrupted its employees and shareholders while driving energy markets into disarray?

Of course, since we met in 2004, Arnold has collaborated with the Democratic California Assembly on some of the most far-reaching and effective energy efficiency and renewables policy in the United States, proving that good energy policy does not need to be (as it has become in Washington) a partisan issue dividing the nation and our people.

As we sat and talked on that winter day in 2004, I presented my idea for how Arnold and I might work together on Western energy policy. We arrived at an agreement. Together, we would propose two goals for Western governors: increase energy efficiency by 20 percent before 2020, and produce 30,000 megawatts of "clean" energy by 2015. We defined clean energy as renewables and coal from which all or most of the carbon is removed and disposed of underground before it can reach the atmosphere.

I believe that we need to push hard for renewable electricity and electric efficiency partly because I want the plug-in car to quickly penetrate our markets, allowing the United States to switch from petroleum to electricity for most of its transportation. That's why a section like this one appears in a chapter about oil and coal. With renewable, sustainable electricity and plug-in automobile technologies, we won't *need* to depend on oil.

Thus Arnold and I set ambitious but achievable goals, and we kicked off a process to figure out the blueprint for achieving them. By June 2004, we had gotten the other governors to endorse the goals in a formal policy resolution and to initiate the single largest policy project in the history of the Western Governors' Association—the clean and diversified energy project. With a lot of help from other Western governors—the standouts included Arizona's Janet Napolitano, Oregon's Ted Kulongoski, Jon Huntsman and Mike Leavitt from Utah, Mike Rounds from South Dakota, and Brian Schweitzer from Montana, a true blend of Democrats and Republicans—we worked up a plan over the next two years.

What we discovered was surprising. We had set our goals too low—despite the objections by Nevada's then governor Kenny Guinn, backed by staff from Colorado's then governor Bill Owens, who said that the goals were too ambitious and unachievable. The region could accomplish much more than we expected, and all quite affordably. I don't want to make the mistake of setting seemingly ambitious but quite meetable goals for energy efficiency and new energy sources again, especially in the context of putting our entire nation on a new and critical energy pathway.

By applying energy efficiency measures to reduce growth in electricity consumption, we would not only prevent the construction of new coal-fired generating plants, we would also save

Western ratepayers about $53 billion over the same period. After 2020, the *annual* savings of these efficiency measures would be about $21 billion. I am going to repeat this kind of information about efficiency several times in this book because the message is so important and so clear. Efficiency puts money in people's pockets—and reduces drag on an economy that needs to stay limber and responsive. Efficiency measures could reduce electric load growth in the eighteen Western states—and the need for huge capital investment in new generating facilities—by about three-quarters, or 75 percent, from 2005 to 2020.

During the Western Governors' Association process, a couple of governors opposed these goals. They said that energy efficiency was unproven. Echoing the rhetoric of some electric utilities that make a profit only when they sell electricity, they said efficiency was too risky.

Behind the scenes, a few coal companies and coal advocacy groups pushed other governors hard to knock down these efficiency goals. It was like a shootout in the old West—white hats and black hats meet at the Old Coal Corral. The coal folks wanted it their way or no way.

Why would coal companies and their allies oppose electrical efficiency? First, coal companies make money when they sell coal. If you make things more efficient—use less electricity made from coal—the companies sell less coal. So protecting profit means opposing efficiency, usually behind the scenes or through allies. That's good for the politicians they support, and it's good for the coal companies, but it's bad for consumers (who run risks of paying high costs to eliminate carbon pollution in the future), and it's bad for the planet.

Why don't all the utilities side with the coal companies? Many do, especially those like Tri-State Electric Cooperative, which provides energy to a number of rural co-ops in New

Mexico as well as Colorado and Wyoming, and Basin Electric, to the east. They are quite partial to coal. But most utilities that are regulated—such as the Public Service Company of New Mexico, or PNM, which has a lot of coal generation but could make a profit without it—aren't as concerned about protecting coal as long as they make money. With decoupling, a policy that allows companies to sell efficiency and price electricity so that pricing encourages conservation, the utilities can make money by being efficient as well as by selling energy. Not so with the coal companies. That is the basic distinction in self-interest that separates the utilities from the coal companies: while the utility market can be restructured to allow utilities to profit from conservation, coal companies can profit only when they sell coal. Efficiency, as well as systems that remove carbon from coal, can raise costs and can force coal to give up market share, so they generally get opposition from coal companies.

Thus, those governors who are the most responsive to the coal companies are the most threatened by efficiency, carbon-clean technology, and renewables. A similar dynamic occurs when we talk about using coal to produce transportation fuel substitutes by a process called "coal to liquids," a proposal that would almost double climate-changing carbon emissions from liquid fuels—the wrong way to achieve energy independence. Coal companies and pro-coal elected officials strongly support coal-to-liquids, and there are very complicated ways to make it climate-friendly. But generally people concerned with climate protection and global warming, as well as development of diverse, reliable energy sources, see that this kind of option requires too much oversight and too much investment to make much sense. We don't need to become more dependent on liquid fuels for transportation. We need to fuel-switch *away* from these options.

We did include coal in the final Western governors' clean-energy report, saying that governors should support projects that made substantial progress toward the goal of removing and burying the carbon from coal before it is used to produce energy. Environmentalists and the coal industry ended up agreeing not that we should continue building conventional coal plants, but that there is an opportunity for new technology to nearly eliminate undesired global warming pollution. That's where our combined efforts need to go for the future of coal. Western utilities are starting to follow up on these recommendations.

The old West needs to give way to the new West, which is heavy with renewable energy potential and doesn't want the mercury and carbon that come with old-fashioned coal.

I don't know whether these coal companies are ever going to change. Look at how Kevin Phillips, a prominent Republican strategist who developed President Nixon's successful Southern strategy that secured the White House for Nixon in 1968, writes about Peabody Coal in the first chapters of his recent book, *American Theocracy*. Phillips starts out with about a hundred pages related to the history of energy policy in the United States, and indicates that the coal companies are heavily supportive of the GOP and have been for the past century. Peabody, for instance, makes relatively huge political contributions. About 5 percent of its profits go to political candidates. Per unit of revenue, this is about fifty times as much as oil and gas or the auto industry. I don't begrudge those contributions or point an accusatory finger. I am just trying to indicate that there's a policy connection between the coal companies and political parties that resists big changes in climate and energy policy.

These companies have fought against any recognition of global warming science or policy. They are pushing back against rules to clean up the air, whether federal or in states like California and New Mexico. When I required Peabody (which was proposing a new coal plant in New Mexico) to submit analysis of carbon-clean coal plant options such as coal gasification in 2003, they submitted, reluctantly and somewhat casually, misleading information indicating that the technology would not be available to produce low- or near-zero-carbon coal plants. (More on that in chapter 5.) Later, they told my staff that they would "never" agree to separate and bury the atmosphere-damaging carbon dioxide associated with coal gasification, because they simply would not submit to such regulation as a condition of building a coal gasification plant. (I don't think I am going to figure large in the political contributions Peabody makes to candidates outside the GOP!)

It may take time, but the facts win out. Our Western Governors' Association report on clean energy and efficiency in the West, initiated and supported by the Richardson/Schwarzenegger partnership (or "Hans and Franz," as my staff called it), was developed by a balanced group of more than two dozen experts from around the region, and in 2006 it was adopted unanimously by the governors. You can find the summary on the Western Governors' Association Web site, www.westgov.org. It's a blueprint for a new clean-energy economy—based on wind, solar, and efficiency—that will benefit Western residents and businesses, and it was prepared and adopted in an open, inclusive, consensus-based process—unlike the National Energy Plan developed by Vice President Cheney in 2001.

Hans and Franz—the Hispanic and the Austrian—somehow won that shootout at the Old Coal Corral. The white hats rode to victory with saddlebags full of efficiency and wind, solar, and geothermal power. And the West, so long considered a reliable defender of fossil energy against all others, is changing into a place where diverse energy sources are appreciated and developed, to the entire nation's benefit.

CHAPTER 4

A Confused World, an Opportunity to Lead

T he Bush administration has supported policies that burn a lot of fossil fuels; it has also burned up the goodwill that citizens of the world once had for the United States.

You can't make everybody happy, but when you make almost everyone unhappy, you shouldn't look as if you're enjoying it. Many around the world have been calling our recent international actions and attitude arrogant. Real leadership is never arrogant. It is inspiring, it is positive, and it is strong—never blind or deaf to the world's concerns as it addresses its own.

One of the great failings of arrogance is its inability to inspire others. Why would the rest of the world want to follow an America that won't inspire, that won't sacrifice? As a nation, we have sacrificed our young men and women in Iraq, but the president hasn't called on the American people to sacrifice in the national interest—the war, for instance, is a credit-card purchase. It's different from the first Gulf War, when we collaborated with dozens of countries to provide armed forces and to join in paying the costs. Sacrifice and inspiration are part of America's image internationally, and that is how we think of ourselves, too. The energy and climate challenge will require that kind of national and international leadership—and a measure of sacrifice and compassion on the part of the American people.

Here's a quick example of what we can do that people around the world will respect.

The United States is often viewed as opposed to and hated by many in the Muslim world. Yet at one point last year, the world's most populous Muslim nation had a strongly favorable opinion of the United States, with polls showing that nearly half its citizens said they liked us.

The world's most populous Muslim nation isn't in the Middle East—it's Indonesia. Indonesians had good reason to like us, since they'd seen, up close, the America that most Americans know and love.

After the devastating tsunami that struck Indonesia and other Pacific nations in late 2004, killing hundreds of thousands throughout the islands and coastlines of the region, we came through for them in many ways: on-the-ground aid from the military, private philanthropy, food and water, and medical assistance. Americans were horrified by what they saw on television, and jumped at the chance to help innocent people in need, without spending a moment thinking, "What's in it for us?" Bipartisan leadership, led by former presidents Bill Clinton and George H. W. Bush, pushed our nation to help, and quickly.

When we hear our nation criticized from abroad, Americans wonder, "How can we be so misunderstood?" We think of the America that wanted to help Indonesia—the one that most of us belong to — and react in disbelief to the anger recently directed at us from abroad. We can't believe what we're hearing.

But over the last few years, when the rest of the world thinks of us, it thinks of a different agenda altogether.

It remembers the Bush administration tossing aside the Anti-Ballistic Missile Treaty and the Nuclear Test Ban Treaty. Our message to the world: we can be trusted to create any kind of weapon of mass destruction we want. Most of the world, I believe, trusts the United States to manage its nuclear arsenal carefully and responsibly, and they recognize the fact that we will control a large arsenal of highly destructive weapons. Yet they also want us to abide by accepted rules for testing, for development of new weapons, for balancing our strength against that of other nations. When we step out of standing agreements and begin developing new weapons on our own, the world loses faith. Why are we the arbiter of who can own or design weapons of mass destruction? People who don't trust the United States can't answer that question. Even people who generally trust us wonder about our motives and self-discipline, in the aftermath of the Iraq invasion and occupation.

Of course, the Iraq fiasco has been hard for much of the world to swallow. We invaded Iraq without the kind of international investment and coalition that had thrown Saddam out of Kuwait in 1991. At the time of our 2003 Iraq invasion, many nations thought we were acting hastily. International weapons inspectors were still at work and had found nothing. We assured the world community that we knew, positively, that we would find weapons of mass destruction in Saddam's Iraq, and as a result the American people stood behind the president. In retrospect, our action seems self-interested and ill-considered. Of course, the loss of life and the destruction in Iraq are seen around the world. Many regard us with a jaundiced eye as a result.

The world also remembers another issue that—like the missile and nuclear treaties—didn't arouse much attention in the United States but seemed huge to other nations sensitive to what they consider bullying behavior. They remember the Bush administration tossing aside the global land mine ban. Our message to the world, again: we can be trusted, and we want all weapons available to us as we need them. The improvised explosive devices that kill so many of our soldiers in Iraq are land mines. So our rejection of the land mine treaty seems to put us in the same category as the people—including terrorists—who would use land mines, even though we say we never will. We did the same thing when we cold-shouldered the international chemical weapons treaty and the International Criminal Court, and when we reinterpreted the Geneva Conventions to redefine torture and confinement of enemy combatants. The world knows about Guantanamo, Abu Ghraib, and the secret U.S. prisons discovered in other countries.

Further, other nations remember the Bush administration walking away from the Kyoto Protocol. Message: before the richest country, the country that most pollutes the climate, will take on the financial burden of lowering its emissions, the rest of the world, especially the poor, must do it first.

The Law of the Sea treaty, still not accepted by the United States, is another example. More than half the world's population lives near coastlines, and billions of people can tell that our oceans are suffering, that they reflect the pollution and overfishing at the hands of larger populations and more sophisticated technology over the decades. Yet the United States has refused to participate in this needed international effort to protect the oceans. It is a further indication, in the minds of those who doubt us, that we are in it for our own good at the expense of others, and that we live by double standards.

In these cases, in just a few short years, the United States went off on its own. There were problems with some of these international agreements. But instead of withdrawing, it is our responsibility—and the world's expectation of us as the world's leading proponent of markets and freedom—to work toward acceptable international arrangements.

While most of the world has reacted in anger and dismay to our new isolation and self-certainty, the right wing and neoconservatives praised the president, saying we were leading the world into a new future. Even a lot of Republicans thought it was crazy. Like most people, they realize that you're not a leader if no one follows you.

I was born in the United States and spent much of my youth growing up in Mexico. I have traveled the world for decades. I studied foreign policy in college and graduate school. I speak three languages (my French surprised my staff and a group of visiting French scientists a couple of years ago), and I have worked and met face-to-face with many world leaders. Because of my experience in Washington and at the United Nations, people from every imaginable country keep in touch with me, even though I am the governor of a small, somewhat isolated state. In fact, as I write these lines, I am returning from North Korea after my sixth trip to negotiate with that nation's leaders on issues that separate the United States and North Korea. Given my background, my interests, and my experience, I don't make the following statement lightly.

I have never seen the United States as isolated, as alone, as it finds itself today.

World leaders are no longer our daily courtiers and contacts. The polls from most nations, including some of our closest allies,

73

show that approval and trust of the United States is at an all-time low—often in the single digits. It's not just that the United States has abdicated its leadership role as the leader of the free world. It's also unsettlingly true that our leaders have alienated people around the world. Polls show that even our longest-standing and closest allies look on us with suspicion.

Still, with the right leadership, this is a situation that shouldn't take long to correct. The American people are full of optimism and ingenuity. The people of the world want to believe that we are responsible and compassionate, that we are committed to freedom and basic rights, and that we want to participate constructively in world affairs. Visionary leadership, and visionary action to implement a new role for the United States, will turn the situation around quickly, and America will find itself surrounded by friends and allies once again.

The key to regaining our leadership role will not be the war on terror, although it is very important, and we must guard vigilantly against enemies who would perpetrate terror against us while we also work with other nations to root out terrorists wherever they are. Nor will the key to new international leadership be trade agreements and economic prosperity, although these are crucial. In this new, uncertain international age, the primary threat and opportunity is the creation of a new energy future that provides hope and prosperity for the United States and other nations while protecting our global atmosphere.

In other words, the way back to world leadership—the necessary and unavoidable way back to world leadership—is for America to combine the issues of energy security and climate protection, to set ambitious goals, and to make their accomplishment the shared priority of leaders in Congress, in industry, and throughout the states. This will, in turn, help spread participation, opportunity, and prosperity across the globe while preventing climate catastrophe.

Some say we're a nation that uses more than its share of resources and gives nothing back. But in fact we are a nation poised to take the lead in conserving resources and in bringing needed technology to the world. Further, some say we're a nation with an agenda that doesn't take the interests of other nations into account. That contradicts our proud history of building peaceful institutions. We know that it's the "big idea"—freedom, or civil government, or fair trade and commerce—that matters, not just at home but around the world.

New leadership will show the world what America is about. We can work our way back to an international polity that considers challenges and needs, and finds hopeful, promising, affordable solutions. We aren't the nation that critics suspect we are, and there may be no better forum than the international energy and climate dialogue to prove it.

As a lifelong student of foreign affairs, and as a public servant concerned about America's role and perception in the world, I have been collecting and analyzing recent headlines that jump out at me. Each tells a story—sometimes a story that's scary—indicating the danger in which the United States has placed itself as well as the danger that overshadows the world when oil and gas supplies are so coveted, and so controlled by a few nations. We need to know the world, in a way the present leadership does not (with disastrous consequences), understand the tensions and issues that influence energy supply and demand, and be realistic about how they relate to international peace and stability. The following examples are particularly instructive and important.

They help explain some of the complexity and difficulty we face in the world today.

"Britain Protests Iran Seizure of Soldiers"
—Associated Press, March 23, 2007

That headline evokes some bad memories for us in the United States. We recall the 1979 hostage-taking at the American Embassy in Tehran, Iran's capital, followed by more than four hundred days of fearful captivity for the fifty-two U.S. hostages, and a period of great anxiety for the nation and concern for the hostages back home.

In this year's case, Iran took fifteen British soldiers and sailors who were patrolling the Persian Gulf. Fortunately, all were released unharmed a couple of weeks later. But during the time that they were in captivity, international tensions grew. Oil markets tightened, and prices rose quickly and sharply. Within a few weeks, gasoline prices in the United States neared three dollars per gallon, a price threshold they had not exceeded since the aftermath of hurricanes Rita and Katrina two years earlier when Gulf of Mexico shutdowns threatened the U.S. market.

In this hostage crisis, diplomacy eventually won out. But you have to ask: Did Iran act to run up world oil prices and make some more money? To divert attention from domestic issues to the international stage? To show a little muscle in the Persian Gulf? We don't know the motives of Iran's leaders, and I would guess that all three possibilities (and others) motivated them.

Regardless of the reasons that Iran acted as it did, there's an energy policy lesson in this episode: we are overdependent on oil, so we are subject to the impacts when world market conditions change. This was a two-week tweak (although prices rose even higher in the summer of 2007, only a few months later). Expert observers say that a longer or more serious episode, involving armies or large attacks or invasions, could cause tensions that would double oil prices, into the range of $120 to $150 per barrel.

Our issues with Iran go deeper than the seizure of British sailors and soldiers, Iran's nuclear program, or the general security of the Persian Gulf. We are concerned about our close ally Israel and about any nation that professes an interest in destroying another. The tensions affecting Israel echo here in the United States.

Iran's oil wealth, burnished by a tight oil market, means that there is plenty of money flowing into Iran both for the government to subsidize low oil prices within the country and for it to support terrorism and hostility in sensitive places and against Israel throughout the Middle East, as well as its nuclear ambitions.

Today some speak of "keeping all options on the table" with respect to Iran, translating to saber-rattling and the possibility of military action against or even the invasion of Iran. We have already had two wars in the oil-rich Persian Gulf region in the past fifteen years, the largest commitments of U.S. force since Vietnam. We can't deny that oil ensnares us.

The March 23 headline about Britain's hostage crisis doesn't directly involve the United States, but the seizure of these soldiers and sailors led to many U.S. headlines about a subsequent sudden, sharp rise in world oil prices. Buyers locked in contracts at higher prices, traders daily negotiated in an atmosphere of uncertainty, and gas-buying Americans heard that any further tension in the Persian Gulf could drive oil prices over $100 per barrel. Here are some contemporary headlines:

"Tensions with Iran Push Crude to Six-Month High"
        —*Boston Globe*, March 30

"Crude Jumps on Rumors about Iran"
        —*Dallas Morning News*, March 28

"What Drove Spike in Crude"
        —*Wall Street Journal*, March 28

There's more to the Persian Gulf than Iraq and Iran, although Americans' attention has been focused on those unpredictable neighboring countries for many years. We have been close to the Saudis for a long time, and they have more oil than anyone else on Earth. Though cautious about appearing to invite American intervention in Arab affairs, the Saudis wanted and needed our help when Saddam Hussein sent Iraqi forces into Kuwait in 1990. The Saudis allowed us to use their territory to prepare the operation to boot Saddam out of Kuwait. Further, they worked closely with our broad international coalition.

They were less enthusiastic about our 2003 invasion of Iraq. At the time they counseled against it—counsel that was ignored. Recently the Saudi king—not a spokesperson, an ambassador, or a prince, but the king himself—denounced the Iraq invasion, war, and occupation ("U.S. Iraq Role Is Called Illegal by Saudi King," *New York Times*, March 29, 2007). Part of his concern is that the Iraq war and civil insurrection have given Shiite Islamists, with close ties to Iran, an opportunity to expand influence and territory to an extent that in Saddam's era was unthinkable.

Wouldn't it be preferable for the United States to achieve a much greater degree of energy independence and be free to base our decisions in this region on strategic aims rather than the threat to our economy if someone shuts down oil supplies? Geopolitically, we've handcuffed ourselves.

We import only about 10 percent of our oil from the region (one reason that the president's commitment to sharply reduce our imports of Mideast oil is relatively empty). Yet we have provided hundreds of billions of dollars in defense of the oil trade in the Persian Gulf. We are going to suffer badly if disruption in this region affects world oil supplies and markets—suffering disproportionate to our actual interest in the region because we are so dependent on oil.

My view is that the United States, in the coming decade, should work closely with Persian Gulf nations from all sides, with our oil-consuming allies, and with the members of the UN Security Council in an effort to create a multilateral security arrangement for the Persian Gulf. No region in the world more demands international attention. No region in the world more demands U.S. attention. And as many observers of foreign policy have recently said, we need to have a dialogue with Iran, not just close our eyes or shake our fists.

It is in the interest of Iran, as well as Saudi Arabia and the other Arab states, to move oil safely through the Straits of Hormuz. It is the one interest, putting aside religious and cultural differences, that might constructively engage these nations with each other. These nations and the oil companies involved in the Persian Gulf oil trade have benefited hugely from the defense of oil reserves and oil transportation routes provided mostly by the United States. We should use the leverage that comes with reduced oil dependence to rationalize—gradually, thoughtfully, and multilaterally—the security of world oil markets and supplies.

"Russian Deals in Middle East Hinder Efforts to Isolate Iran"
—*Wall Street Journal*, February 28, 2007

The subtitle to this front-page headline is "Moscow Sees Market for Arms and Energy; U.S. Protest Is Ignored."

The Soviet empire fell not just because the United States faced it down in the late 1970s and 1980s but also because world energy prices dropped and stayed down, causing privation in the Soviet government, preventing the government from fulfilling its military dreams and even from providing for its citizens.

The spike in energy prices since the end of the twentieth century has certainly changed the situation. Relatively speaking, Russia is rolling in dough—revenue derived from its huge presence in the oil and gas markets. Russia, with massive gas reserves, supplies about half the natural gas used in Europe, where the economy is heavily oriented to natural gas use. In recent years Russia's willingness to change pricing policies, restrict supplies, and negotiate new terms on old pipeline agreements has caused a huge price run-up in countries whose policies Russia does not favor, including some of the now-independent former Soviet satellites. Further, the nations of the European Union (EU) have been negotiating their individual deals with Russia to obtain long-term supplies of natural gas, and as a result Russia has been able to keep the EU at arm's length.

Russia perceives itself as an international superpower, with good reason. According to press reports such as the one in the *Wall Street Journal,* as well as reports from independent media and foreign affairs advisors, Russia also sees itself as a needed global counterweight to the international dominance (and perceived arrogance) of the United States. Russia wishes to diversify and grow its economy, so long suppressed under Soviet rule, and to return profit and gain back to Russia. It wouldn't be the first time, of course. Russia was a world economic power in earlier times, trading and profiting just as European nations and the United States did in the eighteenth and nineteenth centuries.

Thus part of Russia's program is to sell goods into the Middle East, which has the money to buy almost anything. Iran, for instance, is seen by Russia as a good customer.

Why does the fact that Russia is acting in its own interests deserve a huge *Wall Street Journal* story and headline like the one quoted here?

The concern comes from the fact that the area is so dangerous already, and that Russia is using energy to create international leverage in Europe, Asia, and the Middle East. Iran's leadership is unpredictable. The nation has plenty of money and behaves erratically. Its leaders are committed to destroying Israel.

Further, however, Iran has been interested not just in building up its weapons and nuclear technology; it also has another potentially world-changing idea in mind. Along with Qatar, Russia, and some other gas-producing nations, Iran is exploring the concept of an international natural gas cartel, like the oil cartel OPEC. (I warned about this kind of threat to natural gas markets in my 2004 speech to the North American Energy Summit. You can find that speech on my gubernatorial Web site.)

OPEC was formed in the 1960s in part as a response to the fact that President Eisenhower, who was quite an international thinker and had firsthand experience with the horror of world war, had instituted tariffs and quotas on foreign oil in the United States when he saw our imports growing in the 1950s. Our economy was expanding rapidly. The number of automobiles grew exponentially in those years after World War II. This created significant pressure for more oil. As international shipping became more efficient and much safer, it was possible for Americans to obtain gasoline at affordable prices based on crude oil production in oil-rich places across the globe (particularly the Persian Gulf).

So America's foreign oil dependence grew rapidly in the 1950s, a fact that Eisenhower did not miss. He thought a tariff and quota system could help discourage oil imports and, at some expense, encourage domestic production while discouraging profligacy. (The concept of sacrifice in the national interest comes to mind.)

Eisenhower was basically right to be concerned, but the oil-producing nations were also learning and growing. In the early 1960s, a group of them formed OPEC. Within a decade, OPEC leaders applied an oil embargo against the United States (because of our support for Israel) that plunged our economy into a recession, created inflation throughout the economy, caused hours- and miles-long gas lines, and burned itself into the memories of a whole generation of Americans. That was the winter of 1973–1974. A second oil price hike later in the same decade had similar effects.

So discussions among Russia, Iran, and Qatar about the creation of a natural gas cartel should cause some concern. Just as technologies for shipping petroleum changed with the development of supertankers in the 1950s, the growth of liquefied natural gas technology (as well as pipeline technology) has the potential to turn a mosaic of regional natural gas markets around the world into a single global market in coming decades. If the creation of a new international natural gas cartel succeeds, as it well might, the world could be subject to price and supply disruptions and the leverage of natural gas toward politically divisive policies and projects.

What we are seeing now, with Russia taking an aggressive and prominent role in the Persian Gulf, may be a precursor of things to come. Russia's role doesn't stop at providing arms and nukes; Russia is also building relationships that could reshape the global natural gas market. Unfortunately, the United States has been so involved in the Iraq war that it has little flexibility to convince allies to work together on other Persian Gulf and Middle Eastern issues. European nations are particularly unlikely to challenge Russia because of their own energy dependence issues.

I don't see the United States and other powers, even Russia, in bilateral competition. But it is crucial for the United States to act in its own interests and collaborate with its allies, not only to preserve international trade but also to support democracy, civil government, and human rights.

Garry Kasparov, the internationally known chess champion, vigorously opposes the government of Russian president Vladimir Putin. And he thinks the West is rolling over to the detriment of Russia's democracy movement and the West's own long-term interests. He connects the West's failure to stand up for democracy directly to its interests in oil and gas. In March, in the opinion pages of the *Wall Street Journal* ("Putin's Gangster State," March 30, 2007), Kasparov wrote: "This month's flurry of auctions for pieces of the state-controlled Russian energy company Rosneft has attracted an impressive number of A-list banks and Western energy companies. Many reputable corporations seem happy to loot the corpse of [the formerly private hydrocarbon giant] Yukos, the dismembered parts of which are being sold and handed off. . . . The former head of Yukos, Mikhail Khodor-ovsky, sits in prison for not bowing low enough in front of the Kremlin throne."

This passage shows not only that the Russian flair for great lit-erary flourish survives and thrives, but also that Europe and the multinational oil companies might want oil and gas more than they want sustained democratic reforms in the East. It isn't our place to tell Russia how to act, but we can stand up for human rights, as I have throughout my career, and we can pressure com-panies not to behave this way, as we have when we denounce companies who might try doing business in Iran. And above all, we can try to break our own dependence on oil, which has grown so rapidly in recent decades—more than doubling, percentage-wise, since 1979.

How are the oil companies and oil nations who benefit from U.S. protection of the Gulf reacting as Russia flexes its energy muscle? The major oil companies, in the race for oil, are awkwardly placed between large customers and large reserves. BP, Shell, and Chevron—some of the world's largest oil companies—are accepting low-value buyouts of interests and investments they established before the nationalization of oil and gas under Putin. Some are walking away from huge fields that they discovered. Mostly the multinationals are trying to play it slow and quiet, hoping they can get back in and recover invest-ment and make a profit. But as I said earlier, these companies, because they work in a world market, aren't watching out for human rights or U.S. interests. That's the job of our elected lead-ers. We have to do that for ourselves.

Elected officials can watch out for those interests, but they rely on a network of experts to provide information and advice. In the spring of 2007 I saw an obituary for Abe Sirkin, a friend in the State Department who had helped structure much of the United States' human rights policy in the 1970s. I spoke with some of his children about his legacy. He represented what was great about America back at that time—a commitment to helping other nations mature and adopt more democratic policies, and to using U.S. power toward the ideals of civil government. As a young staffer on the Senate Foreign Relations Committee and a recent master's graduate of the Fletcher School of International Diplomacy at Tufts University, I relied heavily on the information and ideas that Abe and several others brought me.

After I was elected to Congress in 1982, I kept in touch with Abe. But it was right around then that our national commitment to democracy-building turned into more of a bilateral contest with the Soviet Union to prevent and check the USSR's potential to reach out in the world. We weren't standing up for freedom as much as were standing up against communism. Both are important, but there's a difference. Do we want to be allied with other nations and lead the international movement toward civil government? Or do we want to be the opponent of communism and nations with whom we struggle for power in a geopolitical chess game? It's never either-or. Yet our progress should always be toward the ideals represented in the Declaration of Independence and the Constitution, the two documents that not only underlie our democracy and institutions but inspire (and have inspired) people around the world.

Today we say that communism is dead, but in actuality it is quite alive and kicking—and successfully teaming up with large corporations—in places like China. I am hopeful that trade will open China to democracy, so I don't oppose that new union. As a nation we have lost our voice for democracy in most places around the world partly because we are so entangled in oil imports. The

Mideast Muslim world in particular regards us with contempt— not that some in that region will ever respect us as long as they follow doctrines of hegemony and hate—seeing us as hypocritical, dishonest, and opportunistic not just because we are Israel's ally but also because we schmooze and befriend nondemocratic nations when they can provide us with oil. We shouldn't and don't live for these people's approval, but neither do we need to give them easy reasons to hate us, to hold our interests hostage, and to call the world's attention to what they consider our hypocrisy.

The Abe Sirkins of our foreign policy establishment, whether in government agencies, the media, or private organizations, help keep us pointed in the right direction. As we reduce our dependence on oil, we should seek out and listen to these voices and forge a new direction for democracy and civil government around the world.

"China Signs On to Tackle Global-Warming Issues"
—*Wall Street Journal*, April 12, 2007

At last, a headline carrying a hint of hope and optimism!

China is both the greatest hope for serious new global progress on energy and climate and potentially the greatest threat to such progress.

Along with ten other major national academies of science (including those of Brazil, India, the U.S., Britain, France, Germany, and Russia), the Chinese science community has signed on to international statements acknowledging the incredible risk of climate change. The Chinese know that drought, famine, sea-level rise, severe weather, and other impacts of climate change would hit China as hard as anywhere else on Earth. In fact, global warming impacts would hit them harder than most, because the Chinese population is the world's largest, and the country is only beginning to build the economic strength and wealth to respond when global warming starts causing major damage and disruption.

China's is a new economy, an economy that is growing fast but struggles to keep up with the understandable demands of its energy-starved people. With more than four times as many people as the United States, China could demand that it should grow to have the same per capita energy consumption and greenhouse gas emissions as the United States. What a horrible situation that would create for people all around the world.

There are few areas in which communism is more efficient than capitalism, but one is ruining the environment. It took the United States' capitalist, free-market economy hundreds of years to achieve the same levels of environmental destruction that China, at its current pace, will achieve in about twenty.

China's economic officials predict that China will build another large coal-based electric-generating unit every week for the next decade. (India is in a similar situation, trying to provide basic electrical service for its own huge population and fast-growing economy.) Why would China decide, on its own, to use more expensive climate-friendly, carbon-clean coal technologies? Especially when it sees the United States refusing to adopt carbon limits and expanding its own carbon emissions every year, even though its economy is relatively mature?

Obviously, the answer is that China won't make a unilateral commitment to the more expensive approach of doing it right. It needs international encouragement, financial assistance, and a commitment that it can grow and provide its people with basic services and resources to build the nation's economy and quality of life. They are 1.3 billion people who are striving to achieve basic human comforts and conveniences of life (which we can sell them, if we get on it). We are 300 million people living in a more mature economy with much higher energy use per capita. Conservatives in the United States who decry any U.S. commitment to cut global warming emissions without a concomitant commitment by the Chinese are demagogues who don't want to solve the problem. The Chinese will likely need to increase, not reduce. While we bring our emissions down, China's emissions will rise. Our goal should be to keep those increases to a bare minimum in a way that helps China join the international economy. That kind of stabilization will be good for the world economy and the world climate.

We absolutely must find a way not only to agree with China and India (and other large, fast-growing nations) on the technologies, energy investments, and emissions limits that will create some future security for our climate, but also to cooperatively make sure that they will have the energy they need.

The only way to get developing nations the power they need, with or without tremendous environmental destruction, is to implement new technologies. We need to expand our energy-producing options, and we need a revolution in energy-*saving* options. We can help China with energy productivity. "China wastes a lot," said the *Economist*'s World Review 2007. "Take energy consumption. China required 4.3 times as much energy as America in 2005 to produce one unit of GDP (gross domestic product), up from 3.4 times in 2002. . . . India, also a rapidly expanding economy, consumes only 61% as much energy as China per unit of GDP." Are China and India following the same fossil energy path to prosperity that the U.S. followed? It appears so. We need to help such nations forge a better path that doesn't threaten the world's basic environmental health.

There's a seamy side to China's economic growth and demand for energy, one that has created incomprehensible suffering and loss.

Although people might not expect the governor of New Mexico to try to resolve the disastrous tribal warfare and genocide in the Sudan, I have been deeply involved. Millions are dying or being forced from their homes. It is an epochal human disaster. China may be the largest international support system that Sudan's leadership can count on to prevent meaningful international intervention. Why? Because China is interested in, and invested in, Sudan's oil. China's insecurity about oil and its energy future is causing it to make alliances with the world's most dangerous and tyrannical dictatorship. The global community and the United States must force China not to coddle Sudan. China will not make that decision on its own because of its energy uncertainties.

China, like most countries, acts in its own interests. So it has pitched to purchase major oil reserves—for instance, the bid to buy Unocal a few years ago. It is a nation growing fast but energy-uncertain. It is an important place for the United States, working with allies, to build relationships and security about world energy supplies and trade.

China needs Mideast oil. It's growing tighter with Iran. One price of this tightness with Iran is that China can't work as cooperatively with Western nations on resolution of Mideast issues, including settling the age-old conflict in Palestine. It might be that those issues are impossible to settle permanently—but we know they are less likely to be settled if members of the United Nations Security Council are tied down by oil alliances throughout the Middle East. We can't even make a decent effort.

It won't be great news to oil-rich nations or the companies committed to an oil-only future, but breaking America's addiction to oil is critical to solving this growing international competition for oil. Preventing similar oil addictions in large, fast-growing developing nations like India and China is the next step.

"Global Carbon Levels Spiraling," reported *USA Today* in a front-page article on May 22, 2007. "Report Points to China's Growth." There's no question about it: the world community, with the United States in a leading role, needs to work out an acceptable energy and climate strategy that allows China to grow, provides mandatory limits to global warming emissions, and allows more and more energy security for countries poor in energy resources—including, increasingly, the United States, as long as we define energy in conventional terms of oil and gas.

I have spent my whole life in diplomacy, working with people, solving problems, from the smallest local issues all the way up to international ones. I keep the door open to talk with people, whether they are hard-core environmentalists or work in the oil and coal industries. (Each of these constituencies sometimes whacks me for talking to the other. Luckily, it's not a *Sopranos*-style whack. But my heart is with long-term sustainability and conservation, renewables, and clean energy, as shown by my high ratings with conservation voters' organizations, such as this year's "A" and last year's "100" from the New Mexico Conservation Voters for my actions on New Mexico legislation.) In this international situation today, we know we have the ability—not just muscle but also ideas and compassion and inspiration—to work with the rest of the world on our greatest challenges, including energy and climate.

No nation is better positioned than the United States—if we are able to break our oil dependence—to lead the world to peaceful resolution of energy tensions and the protection of the global climate. No one else can cut through the chaos and confusion as we can. Diplomacy is key.

CHAPTER 5

Learning from Others

Today's international headlines are about chaos and competition, especially in relation to energy and climate issues. I have discussed the Middle East, Russia, and China, but there are similar headlines around the world concerning Venezuela, Angola, Mexico, and India, to mention just a few.

These countries may not be superpowers, but within those nations the same problems loom. The way different countries are rising to the challenge — or doubling down on the old bad bets — is instructive.

Our nation's relations even with smaller countries that do not rank as economic or military superpowers (as do Russia and China) are overshadowed by our energy demands. Venezuela is a good example. Long an ally and friend of the United States, Venezuela is also a huge oil producer. Now it is ruled by Hugo

Chavez, a leader who holds the United States in the lowest esteem. Chavez aspires to be the successor to Cuba's Fidel Castro—a Fidel with money—as a populist voice countering what he calls American imperialism.

We've been working with other Latin American countries that are producing ethanol, a competing energy source. Brazil has sharply reduced its dependence on oil by enacting a national program to produce oil substitutes, particularly ethanol derived from sugar cane. Colombia, Panama, and Costa Rica also have enacted policies to require ethanol fuel blends and ethanol production. Mexico's growing ethanol supply could displace a large amount of its oil demand and put more of its own oil into play in world markets, increasing revenues. Peru is also moving toward investment in ethanol production.

What I want to discuss here are some exciting examples of new approaches to energy and climate in other nations and in our own states and cities. While we can lead by example, we can also learn from others.

Some of our international allies and trading partners have done truly remarkable things to reduce their dependence on other nations for energy. Let me throw out just a few examples.

Japan has led the world in energy efficiency and conservation. In this case, necessity has been the mother of conservation. "Japan's obsession with conservation stems from an acute sense of insecurity in a resource-poor nation that imports most of its energy from the volatile Middle East. . . . The government in turn has used [energy] tax revenues to help Japan seize the lead in renewable energies like solar power, and more recently home fuel cells" ("The Land of Rising Conservation," *New York Times*, January 6, 2007). As a result, even though average electrical use per household has increased alongside Japan's prosperity since 1980, the average household still consumes less than half as much energy as a household in the United States.

What about China? China's investment in bullet trains is enough to embarrass us in the United States. I have instituted a new commuter train in the central Rio Grande Valley in New Mexico, connecting cities north and south of Albuquerque and now headed toward a long-dreamed-of rail connection between Albuquerque and Santa Fe, about an hour apart by highway. These areas do not have the large metro populations of places like Dallas, Denver, Los Angeles, or Salt Lake City—sprawling Western cities with large metro populations that cynics wrongly said would never support public transportation. (This lack of population density in New Mexico explains why we can't yet afford a high-speed bullet train to connect these metro areas and instead have to rely, to my disappointment, on more conventional trains.)

The New Mexico Railrunner, which runs on conventional tracks that we bought from the Burlington Northern Santa Fe Railroad, has been quite a success. It is subsidized, as all forms of public transportation must be, but it is attracting transit-oriented development nearby as well as large numbers of passengers who welcome the opportunity to commute by rail instead of by individual car. My investment in Park and Ride buses between Albuquerque and Santa Fe, while we work on an efficient rail connection, has yielded standing-room-only ridership.

People who have said that Westerners won't use public transportation are nuts. They are letting old perspectives and political arguments hold us back, while nations like China are speeding ahead with the transportation of the future.

Denmark, a staunch friend of democracy and global markets, has developed and started implementing an energy independence plan that derives a huge amount of energy from wind, but it also goes to the level of using the nation's pig fat as a fuel. France now depends on nuclear power for 80 percent of its electricity, after embarking on a concerted nuclear energy campaign in response to the first OPEC oil embargo. People have their issues with nuclear power, but it is carbon-clean, and the French have embraced it, using safer technologies and storing waste in facilities where it could stay for a few hundred years.

Because of pricing and conservation strategies, combined with the relatively warm winter of 2006–2007, British observers say that electricity demand might be leveling off. *Platt's Electric Power News* reported on March 5, 2007, that Philip Bowman, CEO of Scottish Power, had said, "What we've seen in the UK this year is a reduction in demand—that's probably the first time that's been the case since the first [1973–1974] oil shock." The article indicated that Bowman believes declining energy use in the United Kingdom may force utilities to reevaluate their investment plans. In the United States, it is growing demand that affects investment plans.

European nations are continuing to invest more and more heavily in bike lanes and bike facilities. What a foreign concept—and one that we need to learn from! While Congress is funding "bridges to nowhere" in its huge, pork-laden annual highway bills, cities in Europe are working to get beyond the car culture. It seems inconceivable right now that the United States would implement a truly concerted strategy to get people onto bikes, even though they are healthy, affordable, eco-friendly, and a great alternative to petroleum-powered vehicles. But isn't this something we should consider, along with improved public transportation and more efficient vehicles?

Places like London, Amsterdam, Copenhagen, and Paris have rainy, wet winters, like many of our cities. Yet people bike around and seem happy about it. There are dedicated bike lanes and trails so that riders don't have to worry about car conflicts (just like our Rio Grande Bosque bike trails, which I have expanded—and ridden—during my tenure as New Mexico governor), and there are huge bike parking lots near train stations and commercial centers. This kind of investment makes tremendous long-term sense. I won't accept the cliché that Americans won't ride their bikes to work. If they could do so safely and conveniently, many Americans *would* commute by bicycle quite regularly. It feels great, it's efficient, and if you want to carry a bunch of kids, you can even carpool with the new transporter bicycles being built in Europe—without going to the gas station and without needing a massive investment in a car.

"Oh," the right wing will say, "Richardson thinks we can solve global warming by riding a bike! Ha!" No, I don't think that. But I do think it should be a small but significant step not only in reducing our emissions but also in creating more livable, healthier, and less expensive lifestyles, cities, and energy habits. Maybe our kids will be able to bike to school safely again. Wouldn't that be great? It's the kind of thing that people can't do on their own and that governments should work together to effect. It's not the silver bullet because there is no single silver bullet. We need a set of practical, integrated alternatives to our current situation.

We've fallen behind on international priorities, just as with alternative fuels, alternative transportation, and conservation. There's also the international challenge of global climate change. We have a lot to learn from our European allies on this topic, as well. Former British prime minister Tony Blair spent most of his ten-year tenure expounding on the threat of climate change. German chancellor Angela Merkel, elected in 2005, is quite concerned.

France's new president, Nicolas Sarkozy, though a conservative like Merkel, also considers global warming a central priority.

Maybe instead of saying "we" could learn from our European allies, I should instead say "America's conservatives"— people like Oklahoma senator James Inhofe, who still deny the science of global warming. They could learn a thing or two from European conservatives who want to protect the planet.

Is everything lost with America's right wing? Is there even a glimmer of hope? While I was writing this section, President Bush reversed almost seven years of intransigence on global warming issues by saying he wanted to start up negotiations with fifteen leading nations to reduce global warming emissions.

I was pleased to hear that the president wants to deal with climate change. That was exciting news.

Of course, I was equally surprised and excited when he committed to regulating climate-clogging carbon dioxide under the Clean Air Act as a presidential candidate in 2000. That campaign promise didn't last very long. In retrospect, it appears to have been made as a cynical last-minute campaign gesture to neutralize some of Vice President Gore's support. (People who say W is stubborn and won't change his mind or his policies forget about this one, which was changed with a suddenness that would make your eyes roll around in your head.) Within a few months of occupying the White House, the president had pulled the rug out from under administration people such as EPA Administrator Christie Todd Whitman, who thought it was a real commitment. And then the administration went into a years-long court battle saying it didn't have the authority to manage carbon dioxide, a flimsy legalistic dodge that fell over on itself when the Supreme Court rejected the administration's arguments earlier this year.

But the substance behind the headlines describing the president's new international climate change initiative was vaporous, almost meaningless. In fact, it was worse than meaningless—the president's program (in my view as well as many others') could easily become a distraction that prevents real international progress.

How could that be? It's because the president has stated firmly that he will oppose international or national mandates that would limit emissions. His policy is based entirely on incentives. As such, it is doomed to failure. Incentives are important, but they don't work unless they have some teeth in the form of requirements. That was the experience of the European Union when it adopted voluntary fuel economy standards affecting Europe's car industry. The industry fell far short. Same here in the United States, where overall fuel economy has been stagnant and even declining for the past twenty years, when mandates were left in neutral. People who oppose renewable electricity requirements, like Senator Pete Domenici from my own state of New Mexico, say incentives will work. But incentives (such as the renewable energy production tax credit) have gotten wind and solar energy generation to the point where they command only 1 percent of the U.S. electricity market—not the 30 percent that is necessary for us to begin working toward a sustainable future in the next ten years. Only in the states that *mandate* renewable energy have wind and solar energy exceeded 1 or 2 percent of total electricity.

Industry and investors have little or no reason to buy or produce more efficient technology without the power of mandates. To announce a global warming strategy based on technology and incentives is no more than a dream based in antigovernment ideology.

The president's announcement contained another poison pill. If it could have two deaths, it would.

This second poison pill was arrogance, which has undercut so many U.S. policies as well as our international image since 2001 when this president took office. He included a statement that the United States will now "take the lead" on international policy to combat global warming.

To the dozens of developed and developing nations who have worked hard on this issue, and who have taken it seriously while the United States weakened international scientific reports and abandoned or undermined international negotiations, this was an insult. We have brushed off our closest allies — including, just two weeks before the president's announcement, Merkel and Blair — and now we announce to the world that we expect to take the lead?

If you're going to say you're taking the lead, your plan has to be either the first or the best. You can't show up at someone else's barbecue with a six-pack of cheap beer and tell everyone it's your party. That's one way we could learn from others!

Whether it was his intention or not, the president's gambit takes time and energy away from longstanding, ongoing negotiations at the United Nations, and also takes energy away from European initiatives among the G8 developed nations. Although Chancellor Merkel's response to President Bush's proposal was positive (saying something like "We welcome the U.S. recognition of the importance of this issue"), the German environment minister called it a Trojan horse.

America should become a leader again. It should become the leader by taking important, real steps, by working with others, by producing real solutions.

You don't lead by announcing that you're a leader. You lead by setting the best example.

. . .

The federal government can also learn from the leadership of the states in recent years. Just because America hasn't taken the lead yet doesn't mean we've done nothing. All over America, people are starting to invest in the future.

During the past few years, Americans have become deeply concerned about climate change. While the administration has fought the very idea of climate change, removing references from research and policy documents and earning the concerted response of government whistleblowers, the public has gone in the other direction.

Credit Al Gore, credit states like New Mexico and cities like Seattle, credit California's innovative policies, credit regional efforts like the Western Governors' Association clean-energy project. Also consider that many Americans are concerned about ever-more-devastating natural disasters like Hurricane Katrina. Whatever the reason, the polls show—all over the place, among Democrats, Republicans, and independents, rich and poor and middle-class, in every ethnic group—a very sharp increase in public concern about global warming.

New Mexico, for example, has quickly and comprehensively addressed clean energy, energy efficiency, and climate change. The list of things we have accomplished is long. After eight years of hands-off, libertarian government, we had a long way to go to catch up to other states, and we have done it in a supernova of clean-energy and efficiency policy that kept our legislature, our agencies, our schools, our homes and businesses, and our Public Regulation Commission churning, boiling with new technologies and clean-energy opportunities. Even our utilities have (mostly) started to participate, and some are setting a great example.

What are the states like New Mexico doing?

Energy efficiency   We adopted a law in 2005 that finally required utilities to start planning for energy efficiency. Up until that point, they only made money if they sold power, and the more they could sell (however inefficiently), the better their profit. We changed the law to say that they could increase rates if they also saved energy — usually a net savings to the customer *and* the utility.

Green building   We adopted rules that require state agencies to use green building practices that may cost a little more but save money and energy in the long run. Further, we enacted a set of tax credits for private builders to make it worthwhile for them to invest a little more in construction so that their buyers would save money and energy over time. Now we are revising statewide building codes to integrate green building practices into construction and remodeling.

Renewable energy   We instituted, then doubled, a requirement for utilities to use renewable power, now requiring 20 percent renewables by 2020. (We could do a lot better with a federal law requiring more. It's hard for states to do this on their own.) Also, we have enhanced the federal renewable energy production tax credits, encouraging more renewable energy development in our wind-rich state. And we will stimulate renewable energy development with a new Renewable Energy Transmission Authority that will help energy developers ship their power to hungry markets — and will help plan and finance the energy storage options that will allow wind and solar to become baseload energy resources available anytime.

Transportation   I mentioned earlier that we funded a new commuter rail line that will soon connect Albuquerque and

Santa Fe. Further, we eliminated the sales tax on hybrid cars, saving each buyer about $700 right at the dealer (instead of having to wait until tax season for a tax credit). I have supported planning for light rail and bus rapid transit in our major cities, as well as lots of new bike trails.

Renewable fuels   We have instituted a requirement that will make biodiesel a higher percentage of diesel fuel sales in New Mexico, and we are pushing for infrastructure that will help customers buy gasoline that contains higher percentages of ethanol. In the meantime, our biofuels production capacity has quintupled, including increasing the capacity of our first biofuels plant, managed by Abengoa in Portales, by tens of millions of gallons a year. Other, even larger biofuels facilities are now starting up.

Incentives   I might have been the first person ever to utter the words "distributed generation"—the concept of allowing customers to generate their own electricity instead of buying electricity from central generation plants owned by the utilities—on CNN's *Larry King Live* show, back in 2003 after the huge electrical blackouts in the East and Midwest. I am working to make "distributed generation" happen here in New Mexico. We quadrupled the federal solar incentives for installing solar collectors at your home or small business, as well as for solar hot water heating. We also changed the rules governing how utilities buy back customer-generated power, creating a much larger opportunity for people to sell their extra solar and wind power back onto the grid while reducing their own power bills.

Overarching climate change action   I adopted strict targets to reduce greenhouse gas pollution from New Mexico and started up an advisory group to educate me about the most important measures for meeting targets. Later, I adopted all of the group's recommendations, starting with reducing the escape of natural gas from pipelines and wellheads. Raw, unburned methane is far more destructive in the atmosphere—about twenty-three times more destructive than carbon dioxide—so as a natural-gas-producing state, we can prevent a lot of damaging emissions by requiring gas producers and pipelines to tighten up their development. Of course, the producers make money because they aren't wasting gas, and eventually the state will receive royalties on gas that had previously escaped into the atmosphere. Further, in the absence of federal climate policy, I have pushed hard for a regional agreement to firmly limit emissions among a group of Western states.

That's the short list. There's lots more. But the point is, a federal government (and a president) interested in the issue will do well to learn from states and cities. In fact, it would be smart to give states and cities incentives to do more, through a set of federal Climate Challenge block grants that reward innovation and local solutions all over the country. That will be part of my program.

America can also learn from others by what they do to address real proposals for energy development. Some conventional energy development proposals, unfortunately, still fly in the face of our goals regarding climate protection, efficiency, and clean-energy development. Governors (and presidents) sometimes need to choose between directly opposing goals. Here is another example from New Mexico.

I adopted strict targets and programs to reduce global warming emissions in New Mexico, but we still had a couple of conventional coal plant proposals on the boards. Most elected officials figure they need to support economic development proposals, no matter how they may conflict with global warming goals. Especially in the West, where coal has been king, those proposing conventional coal plant development have counted on a governor's support and expected that global warming reductions would be put aside in favor of economic development. Not so in New Mexico, and I take some credit for changing that dynamic in the West overall. Until I stood up to Peabody Coal's proposal for a coal plant called Mustang and pushed the clean-energy project through the Western Governors' Association, there hadn't been a governor in the Mountain West who had taken such strong stands in recent years.

Talking about climate change and global warming in a state like New Mexico used to be considered politically risky. When I was elected, it was common wisdom that the governor of such a state, which some wrongly consider a mini-Texas, should not take on issues such as climate change and clean energy. But I had campaigned on a platform including climate change policy, and I intended to follow up on it.

To address climate change in New Mexico, I ordered an interdepartmental analysis to figure out what kinds of impacts global warming would create, such as increased wildfire and drought, and then I started talking to people about them. My administration put out a report about the impacts of climate change on New Mexico, which achieved national attention. In fact, it received attention in a way that forty-nine other governors would have loved.

We issued the report at the end of 2005, in accordance with my climate change executive order. In February 2006, the report was front-page, above-the-fold news in USA Today ("America's newspaper"). But there's more to the story. USA Today's coverage occurred during the middle of the National Governors' Association (NGA) annual meeting in Washington, D.C. Staying at the Willard Marriott Hotel on Pennsylvania Avenue, I imagined forty-nine other governors opening the door to their rooms that morning and picking up *USA Today* to see the front-page story on global warming featuring New Mexico's leadership and its report on climate impacts in our state. That kind of recognition gives a governor a warm feeling inside, carbon-free. (Competition among governors is not a bad thing. Governor Schwarzenegger and I jockey for leadership on climate and energy issues. I certainly claim the title of being the most aggressive and effective clean-energy governor of an energy state, and with 37 million green Californians behind him, Arnold can claim other leadership titles.)

I don't do these things for the publicity—I do them for the impact. But what governor wouldn't want to be featured that way at the heart of the NGA annual meeting?

When people in New Mexico saw that climate report by our agencies, they were concerned. They knew intuitively that our nation's energy policies—even though they create great revenue and fiscal benefits for a state like New Mexico—are shortsighted and blind to issues such as climate change. They saw the Bush administration trying to drill for oil and gas everywhere, even in ecologically precious places like New Mexico's Valle Vidal and Otero Mesa, where hunters and ranchers, conservationists and communities are all concerned about the administration's intense interest in more, more, more. They wanted us to set a different course, with more renewables, more efficiency, new types of vehicles, and new programs to get carbon out of coal.

I have put New Mexico's policy where its mouth is at an administrative level, too, opposing energy projects that threatened our goals of sustainability and a new energy economy. I adopted an executive order directing our agencies and administrative boards to protect the resources of the federal land at the Valle Vidal. This area—home to one of the state's largest elk herds, with world-class fishing and a gentle mountainous beauty that remains largely untouched—was targeted for energy development not just by the U.S. Forest Service but by the White House. Newspaper stories indicated that the White House staff had been in direct contact with local Forest Service managers, telling them that El Paso Natural Gas (another big supporter of the Cheney/Bush energy strategies) wanted to drill there.

I objected. I went up to the Valle Vidal and had my picture taken with several dozen local hunters holding their guns (unloaded, if my security team did its job) and wearing orange hunting vests. This land was donated to the Forest Service by Pennzoil in 1982 for perpetual conservation. Although it is adjacent to a large ranch controlled by Ted Turner that uses model natural gas production practices (Ted can't deny access to the subsurface because it is separately owned under federal leasing practices), the Valle Vidal is public land that doesn't need pipelines, roads, and toxic drilling materials in pits all over the place. Natural gas production necessarily includes widespread, intensive impacts on the surface of the land—not just the well pads, as some would have you believe. The Valle Vidal, a New Mexico treasure, is an area deserving protection—the kind of protection that only Congress can give, but a governor can stimulate.

So I started a successful campaign to designate Outstanding National Resource Waters on the Valle Vidal, preventing stream degradation.

I instructed our state engineer not to allow wells, and our oil and gas officials not to allow pits for drilling wastes.

I told our environmental officials that I wanted road proposals to be challenged and prevented.

I held public events with advocates of conservation, even though people in the industry grumbled that I was supporting "no-growth wackos."

I proposed and enacted policies that would reduce natural gas use far more than the Valle Vidal could provide.

And I submitted a petition to the Forest Service telling them to permanently designate this area as "roadless" and closed to development, an addition to the roadless lands the agency had designated in the 1970s. That was clever: I was also opposed to the Bush administration's roadless policies, but since the Agriculture Department had announced that they wanted the governors' petitions for which of the designated roadless areas should be protected permanently, I sent one in and included an area they hadn't been considering!

By December 2006, as the Democrats were poised to take control of Congress, the assiduous efforts of conservationists, hunters and anglers, and the state paid off. Senator Pete Domenici finally agreed to support protection of the area and, with Senator Bingaman and Congressman Tom Udall (a Democrat representing northern New Mexico), sent a bill protecting the Valle Vidal to the White House for the president's signature. Bingaman and Udall had been on board with this proposal for years, so they didn't mind letting the Republicans take credit— they just wanted the place protected.

It was a huge victory for New Mexico, and a signal to others throughout the West: with gubernatorial leadership and hard work in Congress, we might be able to protect these areas we love from rampant energy development.

I know the nation looks on the West as an energy breadbasket. But even though the nation needs energy, there are standards we must uphold and places we must protect. And we must change our energy habits, not just exploit everything everywhere.

This is what Vice President Cheney and President Bush simply do not understand after so many years on private ranches and in corporate boardrooms. Certainly, I have spent time on private ranches and in corporate boardrooms. But as you can see by my actions and my proposals for the nation's energy future, I haven't let those experiences crowd out my awareness of balance and the need for sensible long-term policy for our energy needs, our public lands, and our communities.

It doesn't stop with oil and gas, however. I have also been willing to stand up to proposed coal projects in New Mexico—an example that the federal government and the White House could learn from.

When Peabody Coal proposed a conventional coal-electricity-generating plant in western New Mexico, I told our Environment Department to require analysis of a potentially carbon-clean coal alternative known as IGCC (or integrated gasification combined cycle), which allows carbon emissions to be captured prior to combustion and buried underground. Even though my main emphasis for the United States is on renewables and efficiency for our future, I believe these near-zero-carbon coal plants are going to be important around the world, but, unfortunately, the industry hasn't embraced them yet.

I'm not anti-coal or anti-Peabody. This is just one story. And Peabody is just one of many companies that have not yet envisioned change or embraced change and that may be very much opposed to change.

Grandstanding about the evils of energy companies is an easy road to choose politically, but it's not the easy road to changing our energy problems. When I say we're all in this fight together, I'm talking about companies like Peabody, too.

Change is needed quickly, not only for the sake of the atmosphere or the scions of industry, but for the workers in coal states
whose very livelihood depends on a thriving coal industry. We
have a lot of coal in New Mexico. I am not opposed to developing it. I want to help create jobs and opportunity for people — but
I want it done right.

The apologists for the coal industry who accept all industry
proposals without analysis (and according to Wall Street analysts
there are fewer and fewer such unconditional apologists) are not
doing anyone any favors. Their shortsightedness will end up
doing more to hurt the coal industry than those who favor
change. In fact, if and when market-based carbon controls come
into effect and create a cost for carbon emissions, these facilities
will face the largest cost risk of any. That will hurt the utilities
that control them, as well as the coal companies that supply the
coal. As Senator Bingaman and California senator Barbara Boxer
made clear in an opinion piece in the *Dallas Morning News* in
the spring of 2007, there should be no special treatment (such as
grandfathering) for companies that rush these plants into construction and production before carbon controls take effect.

Let me say more about Peabody's proposed Mustang
electricity-generating plant in New Mexico. The company strongly
resisted our requests for information on IGCC, offering handwrit-
ten technical submissions that dismissed the possibilities for
IGCC. Peabody didn't take our requests seriously, waiting months
and months between submissions (as mentioned on page 66).

We were the first state to make that kind of best-available technology requirement for IGCC analysis by companies proposing
conventional coal plants. A few other states gradually followed suit.
The Bush administration's Environmental Protection Agency
(EPA), in its continuing war on states with progressive environment and climate policies, backed Peabody. In December 2004,

the EPA even issued a policy letter saying that states could not require IGCC analysis as "best available control technology" alternatives to conventional coal plant proposals, as New Mexico had done. (They later withdrew this policy directive, under pressure from environmental lawyers, as it clearly went against the spirit and letter of the Clean Air Act.)

To my disappointment, Peabody Coal eventually withdrew its application for the Mustang plant (although they proceeded to open a mine in accordance with mining law and ship the coal elsewhere, showing the importance of regional and national carbon-control mandates, not just state-by-state action). I wish the company had seen the significance and value—and the state's potential financial and political support—of a carbon-clean coal facility in this area, where people need jobs. But the company and much of the coal industry apparently see a threat to their existing business model if they embrace IGCC and other gasification technologies that could be a bridge to widespread adoption of IGCC technology. I believe we could have resolved Peabody's concerns regarding the power reliability and cost of IGCC. It would have taken cooperation and vision on both sides, but I know we could have done it. And we could have shipped the carbon dioxide out in nearby CO_2 pipelines controlled by international pipeline giant KinderMorgan that help enhance oil recovery in the Permian Basin to the south. It would have been an example for other states, and the feds, to learn from.

I had met with Peabody Coal earlier in my administration. I have always worked well with energy industry people, from my earliest days in Congress. But I had to discourage Peabody, in my first days as governor, from opening a large coal project that the Hopi people, the Navajos, and the Zuni Pueblo saw as a major threat to the water table of their sacred Salt Lake, also known as Fence Lake, in western New Mexico. The tribes had traditionally put aside their differences—not inconsiderable, given some of the land disputes and history among them—when it came to the lake so that their people could gather needed salt as well as worship.

When I became governor, that Peabody proposal for a coal operation at Fence Lake had been in administrative proceedings for years. Native American representatives had attended administrative hearings held by an earlier administration on the proposed mine, which would have included a major slurry operation to get the coal to where it could be transported by rail. The story of one of these administrative proceedings made its way back to me on the East Coast in late 1996 or early 1997.

This particular hearing, held as I recall in October 1996, included testimony by elders who had never before left their native lands, even to come to Santa Fe. They spoke no English, but their testimony was a vivid reminder that when we produce energy—energy that is demanded in our ever-hungry system—we can mean a lot more by "environmental impact" than just climate change. Major projects have an effect on the people who live near them, and their voices must be heard as well. (Certainly this is true of the devastating impacts of mountaintop removal mining in Appalachia and gigantic surface mines in the coal-rich Powder River Basin of Wyoming and Montana.)

At this administrative hearing one of the tribal elders held up a bag of salt from Fence Lake, saying that it was sacred. Further, he said in his native tongue, with a pause for translation into English so that the lawyers, the administrative judge, and the observers could understand, the salt had been chemically analyzed and found to contain lithium. This, he explained slowly and gently, had perhaps contributed to his people's widely recognized calmness.

He quietly recommended that the opposing lawyers try some. As the translation of this wry statement reached the audience, there was laughter in that hearing room, even among the company's lawyers. It was a comical moment, but it reflects the feeling of relief that the tribal peoples shared when Peabody backed away from developing the coal near Fence Lake after meeting with me in my first months as governor.

I want to see coal as a part of our energy future, and I know it can play an enormously valuable role. To achieve this, we need to embrace new technologies in coal, just as we do in automobiles. We can't keep providing energy from conventional technology. Continuing to construct conventional coal facilities without carbon controls only dooms those facilities to the economic risk that they will have to pay a large price to continue emitting carbon when we create a carbon cap and market for trading and selling carbon rights. Carbon controls are absolutely necessary to make sure that coal companies and others comply with the goal of cleaning up the atmosphere.

It is a sad commentary on the state of affairs that the coal industry's support for these new technologies is limited to a few cases, such as the Bush administration's proposal for a single huge IGCC demonstration project called FutureGen. That project seems to me to be a ruse, a platinum-plated diversion, which will take years and years to get going and will probably end up lagging behind the market. Notably, a few adventurous utilities, such as Excel in southern Colorado, are proposing faster, less expensive IGCC options that will leapfrog FutureGen.

Many in this debate try to set up the argument as anti-this and pro-that. The only position that matters is whether you're ready for the future or not.

The coal world, to continue with this example, would do better to accept government incentives, like those I have enacted in New Mexico, to put carbon controls in place and to build a fleet of coal plants that will be able to survive and thrive in the carbon-constrained world we know is right around the corner.

How do these experiences with Peabody and El Paso in New Mexico relate to global warming and climate change policy, nationally and internationally?

First, they indicate that energy policy is also sometimes a proxy for other concerns—not just global warming, but social and cultural and local impacts of our energy production system and how we use energy. Using less, using diverse sources, and using wisely are all important not just to protect the climate, but to consider the needs and interests of real people in real places. Second, these experiences show that climate change and energy policy can be important and effective even against the opposition and leadership of the federal government and superpowers in the energy industry. I want those energy superpowers, from Peabody to Chevron, to be full participants in our energy, security, and climate revolution. They can still profit, and they can still provide needed energy to the world—but they can do it in a fashion that takes long-term interests into account. And third, they show that the federal government has much to learn from other nations and from our own states.

The Valle Vidal story and the two Peabody stories—Mustang and Fence Lake—hold a larger message. They lead toward the conclusion that we need to respect the environment and respect communities, not just suck their energy out and use it somewhere far away. Further, we need tough national and international standards to control carbon emissions and force change in the energy industry. States can't adopt these standards on their own—even a gargantuan economy like California's needs controls across a larger market or it simply drives business (and pollution) to other places. And sometimes we need to stand up to industry, not just roll over.

We also urgently need to push forward with implementing new central solar technologies, as California, Nevada, and Spain have been doing. These technologies produce steam heat to drive turbines, and their ability to store midday heat (in molten salt, for instance) and release it a few hours later is perfect for meeting summertime, late afternoon peak demand. It's an option for states like Arizona and New Mexico to provide plentiful power for the whole Western grid. We have been looking for a good solar project like this one to start up in New Mexico. I know it will happen soon, especially with federal support.

Learning from others is something the current administration doesn't understand, but these are lessons and messages I have learned well. They lead me to the conclusion that we need those controls and mandates, and we need a diverse, energy-efficient economy. It might cost a little more at first, but if the federal government is helping the way states have been doing, the costs will quickly come down.

CHAPTER 6

The Costs of Action, the Price of Inaction

O scar Wilde, the English playwright, said, "A cynic is someone who knows the price of everything, and the value of nothing."

Cynics about climate change and new energy—people who don't believe that climate change is happening, that we are contributing to it, or that we can afford to make changes—certainly have not considered the price of inaction. Likewise, I don't believe they have fairly considered the actual, affordable costs of developing and implementing alternatives to oil and coal.

Americans pay the price of inaction on energy policy every day, at gas pumps and utility bill-paying counters. As sea levels rise, droughts extend, and famine and disease spread in unpredictable ways, they will pay the price of inaction on climate change sometime in the future. Sadly, future generations in particular—people who can't vote or speak up today—will pay the price for that cynicism so characteristic of the president's and past congresses' energy and climate policies. Cynics ignore the value of a healthy environment, of a diverse and competitive energy economy, and of converting petrodollars to local jobs and energy. They ignore the value of energy efficiency, both in saving money and energy today and in protecting against higher price spikes that could occur in the future. Worse, they advance policies that are at best half measures and at worst, diversions from the real change we need. I look at the 2005 Energy Policy Act. As I have said, it was a gift to existing industry and ignored or underplayed the importance of alternatives. I look at the administration's continued war on efficiency and alternatives in the trenches of budgets and agencies—eliminating regional efficiency offices, unsuccessfully contesting efficiency standards (which I adopted as energy secretary) in the courts, placing oil and gas development as the highest priority for management of our public lands. I look at the 2007 Energy Policy Act that just passed the U.S. Senate—better, but still a baby step compared to what we really need.

We can't afford this cynicism. We can't afford to listen to these Chicken Littles who run around saying the sky *isn't* warming. We need to learn from our allies, learn from our cities and states, and lead by example. We need to be willing to pay the costs of acting now, so that we don't later pay the much higher price of inaction on energy policy and protecting the climate.

Energy efficiency, or productivity, is a natural result of higher energy prices. Throughout the markets, people and businesses learn to operate more efficiently. They spend a little more to buy more-efficient machines, appliances, and buildings, and they reduce energy-consuming activities that they can cost-effectively live without.

Energy efficiency is also a great example of how the cost of acting now might seem high, if you are counting on a quarterly reporting system or if you are an agency or a household working on a set budget. But the ultimate price is much higher if you don't adopt efficiency measures. A little up-front investment goes a long way, producing value in cost savings, energy savings, and climate protection. I saw many a cynic oppose the Western Governors' Association's proposed efficiency goals, but the argument that we'd save a lot more in the long run always beat them.

It is truly surprising how much more efficiency we could wring out of our economy—and the global economy—while saving a lot of money overall. Efficiency is a huge, readily available energy resource. But most utilities, for instance, don't make money selling efficiency. They make money selling power.

As I wrote in chapter 5, we changed that in New Mexico a couple of years ago. The New Mexico Legislature adopted my proposal to allow utilities to sell slightly higher-cost power to fund efficiency investments that would in turn obviate investment in new generating facilities or contracts. This saves both the consumer and the utility money that would have gone into the capital and fuel costs of new electricity generation. Further, it is critical to "decouple" utilities' ability to make money so that they can offer efficiency services and make an acceptable rate of return not just by selling natural gas or electricity, but also by selling the services that help consumers reduce their demand.

In a 2007 report on global energy productivity, the McKinsey Global Institute (MGI) found that practical, cost-effective energy productivity investments could cut new worldwide energy demand in half over the next fifteen years. The research indicated that these investments would pay an internal rate of return of 10 percent or more. Around the world, energy demand will grow by 2.2 percent annually without these efficiency investments, according to MGI, far faster than the 1.7 percent annual growth since 1986. Eighty-five percent of this growth will occur in rapidly developing economies—about one-third in China alone. With sensible, cost-effective efficiency programs, this growth will be cut in half, the equivalent of about 64 million barrels per day of oil—or about three times as much energy as the United States uses in oil every day.

In other words, by saving money that would have paid for new generating facilities and fuel needed to provide the same amount of energy, efficiency investments don't cost, they pay back. And as MGI points out, the money not spent on wasted energy is money that can be put toward other types of consumption or investment, creating economic return for individual businesses, nations, and the world economy.

This is why I reject the car companies' and oil companies' arguments that higher fuel economy raises costs for customers. Standard and Poor's recently said that my proposal to sharply increase fuel efficiency to 50 miles per gallon by 2020 would add as much as $6,000 to the cost of an average car. First, I think that number is wildly inflated. The $6,000 figure is scary—but wrong. But even if it were accurate, getting twice as many miles per gallon equates to a great fuel (and money) savings for the driver. That fuel savings, with prices around where they are today, would keep about $1,000 in the average driver's pocket every year. Those who travel more would save even more. And if fuel prices go up and up, the savings would be even greater.

Even if it did cost $6,000 more for the car, and then $6,000 less for gas, that would mean a lot of extra money going to American auto workers, instead of the oil-controlling nations and companies. Americans need to start thinking that way. You can call it sacrifice, or investment, or robbing Osama to pay Paul, but it's the mind-set we must have. We should invest in ourselves instead of in the oil industry and oil despots.

In my administration, we will implement federal rebate programs to soften the consumer impact of buying highly efficient cars and trucks, so that average consumers will not have to pay all those up-front costs, and I will also offer financial assistance so that automakers can retool (or start up) at lower cost.

As our country reduces its dependence on foreign oil, we will also be able to save some defense funding now dedicated to keeping the world's oil fields and oil transportation routes safe. This must be done safely and carefully, in concert with other nations, and will not occur quickly. But over time it will create significant, valuable savings in our economy and our federal budget—money that can be used more productively in paying off debt, helping make the economy more efficient by supporting health care for all, improving educational opportunities, and putting new sustainable energy options and energy efficiency measures in place. Efficiency includes smart defense spending.

Japan has built an enormously efficient economy—according to MGI it is three times as efficient as the global average. It is important to recognize that Japan has fewer energy resources available than does the United States, and that much of the Japanese population lives in highly concentrated urban conditions and small homes that the average American wouldn't accept. All the same, we can see that energy efficiency is not incompatible with real economic growth and progress. The emphasis on energy efficiency pays back double when energy prices rise sharply, as they have done recently. Not only does Japan save on fuel and energy costs, but it also has a technology

123

edge in world markets. Automobiles are a good example. Look at how Japanese automakers have recorded strong profits worldwide (including in the United States) as energy prices have risen and consumers have purchased more efficient vehicles.

Efficiency investments don't come automatically. Let's look specifically at the building sector.

Residential energy demand is the largest worldwide, constituting 25 percent of world energy demand, according to MGI. Available technologies alone could reduce this sector's annual demand growth from 2.4 percent to 1 percent. By available technologies, MGI means efficient lighting, efficient building-shell construction (insulation, materials, windows, and doors), and efficient water and space heating. These savings also translate to savings in the energy sector itself, which has to produce that much less energy. If these available techniques are employed, "green building" could eliminate 5 percent of global energy demand by 2020.

It's easy for someone not versed in this to get lost in the numbers and in the vague term "technology." But using "available technologies" is the equivalent of switching from a gas-guzzling 1993 Buick Park Avenue to the Prius. It's easy to forget how much of our energy is lost on things—houses, cars, factories, office buildings—that were built comparatively long ago.

Changing over to already existing efficiency technology would create a huge amount of saved energy, and from that time forward the savings would continue to build up.

The first obstacle to this kind of savings is that builders aren't accustomed to using these technologies. In my home state of New Mexico, the homebuilders in the Albuquerque region (our largest metro area) are interested in green building, but they don't know a lot about the techniques, they don't have time to learn the new techniques, and they put themselves at a price disadvantage if they spend extra money on building techniques or materials that other builders don't use. People choose houses on price, not on the prospect of lower utility bills.

All the same, the head of the Albuquerque homebuilders' association, Jim Folkman, recently wrote an opinion column about the importance of these changes. He sees the potential impact of climate change not only on the world, but also on New Mexico, where drought cycles and temperatures are projected to intensify. We could lose our ski industry. Our agriculture will change. Water supplies will be harder to manage and potentially much lower. Folkman, like responsible citizens all over the country, sees that "something is happening." He's a good example of someone in an existing industry who wants to change but needs education, technical support, and programs that will help the shift.

In the policy world, we are edging closer and closer to building codes and other requirements (including smart-growth and transit-oriented development programs that result in higher-density development nearer to public transportation) that will make it every builder's job to create a more sustainable residence or workplace.

At present, we have numerous incentives that direct investment the wrong way. In the residential sector, we offer mortgage support for homes based on the housing cost alone. Banks that do that ignore the huge household costs of transportation that families will carry by purchasing a less expensive home miles and miles away from jobs, schools, and shopping.

Many suburban commuters know what I am talking about. As interest rates rise (especially on adjustable-rate mortgages) alongside gasoline prices, commuters are pressed from both sides. High gasoline prices *and* suburban development patterns without public transportation options help explain high bankruptcy and foreclosure rates. As gasoline prices rise, these costs become unbearable for many households in far-flung new suburbs. In many jurisdictions, such as Detroit and Houston, even with the lower energy costs of a few years ago, the household investment in daily transportation by private automobile exceeded the household's investment in housing.

Think of the time we waste driving around, not just the money wasted, the energy imported from other countries, and the emissions of fossil carbon that are changing the climate. Instead of spending time at home with the kids, people have to drive them all over the place. I sometimes lose staff people who love the work in my office but just can't do all the driving and oversight of kids as well as pull a seventeen-hour work day. (Only joking!) It's hard to live in many of these new residential developments without jumping in the car and driving a zigzag to get to stores, workplaces, hospitals, music lessons, soccer games, schools, and entertainment. It's life in the car.

Further, we allow depreciation of building investments on a thirty-year schedule, "devaluing investments in energy efficiency," according to Lisa Margonelli at the New America Foundation, a policy organization that sponsored the public rollout of my energy and climate policy in May 2007. And our tax code allows the owner of a commercial building to write off the entire energy bill—giving the landlord a reduced incentive to invest in new efficiency measures, and giving the tenant virtually no incentive to turn down the thermostat.

A special report ("Less Power to the People," *Wall Street Journal*, October 16, 2006) identified ten areas where we can make huge advances in energy productivity. The list started with lighting. If everyone in the country replaced a conventional lightbulb with a new fluorescent bulb, consumers would save about $600 million (or $2 for each bulb) in energy costs every year. Multiply that by the number of bulbs in a full household (recognizing that some bulbs are used more than others), and you can see that there are potentially tens of billions of dollars in annual savings waiting out there. Moving to a diode, or LED, which is still relatively expensive, saves 92 percent of the energy used by a conventional bulb. As lighting technology continues to improve, we will save more and more energy—and money.

I wish the industry would come up with new, short, sharp names for some of these needed technologies and efficiencies. The phrase "compact fluorescent light bulb" (CFL) is itself enough to scare people away. It's too long. It includes the word "fluorescent," reminding people of deadly windowless high-school study halls instead of invoking the soft, pleasant light of the new CFL. And why use a phrase like "light-emitting diode" (LED)? Does anyone on Earth know what a diode is? Probably someone at the two national labs in New Mexico, but not me! And probably not you! But I love the bright light, the lower temperature, and the 92 percent energy savings.

Lighting is a good example of the efficiencies that are available today but that require consumers and builders and utilities to implement them, and require education and financing for people to adopt them.

Efficiency investments reduce costs to consumers and create a much more productive, efficient economy. The New America Foundation reports that an electrical consumption standard for battery chargers used, for example, in cell phones and laptop computers would save consumers $2 billion per year, and that California's efficiency standards, adopted in recent decades, provide the average California household with $400 to $1,000 savings per year—savings that can be applied to other consumption or to investments that can pay a higher or longer return than a utility bill. Plasma televisions are the fastest-growing new energy consumer. We should encourage efficiency in that kind of new market, too.

There's little question that inefficiency is more expensive, costing more than efficiency in the long run by hundreds of billions of dollars. The cost of efficiency is worth it. Efficiency pays well and it pays fast. It's the first cost we need to be willing to pay, while expecting a respectable return on our investment. Conversely, the price of inefficiency is huge: vulnerability to price spikes for fuels such as oil and gas and coal, worsening climate conditions, and hundreds of billions of petrodollars exported every year. The value of efficiency should be recognized, along with some mandates that will continue to push our economy to much higher levels of efficiency.

We need to build a market in which it costs to emit global-warming pollution. We need to create a real market cost for the now-ignored costs to society when a carbon emitter produces global warming pollution.

Markets matter. They serve and guide us every day. We need to create and manage a new carbon market.

Right now, carbon emissions have no economic consequence, except to benefit the individual emitter who sells a product or service. In that sense society is subsidizing not only climate change but the emitter's individual business decision. There is no price for emitting climate-changing gases. Thus the atmosphere, and the climate, have no value in a business sense.

The formula needs to be reversed. Carbon emissions must cost the emitter. Once this basic step is taken, there will be a different type of economic and financial race—no longer a race to the bottom, a race to produce and sell more products regardless of their carbon impacts, but instead a race to find the best, most-affordable options that reduce carbon emissions.

To meet this goal of representing the costs of carbon pollution in the marketplace, I propose the concept of a "carbon auction." Most of the details described next would be subject to discussion with Congress and the regulated community, but the tenets are simple: it will cost to emit carbon, and the aggregate amount of carbon pollution rights offered at auction will diminish from year to year.

Now a few slow paragraphs to explain the concept of a carbon auction. Hang on tight. I love policy change and new directions, but policy itself can swallow you whole. (Maybe that's why so many of my policy advisors look as though a whale just spat them out!)

The first step will be for the government to firmly establish the baseline—how much global-warming pollution are we creating today? Some of the answer to this question is going to have to come from complicated modeling, as Congress has still not been able to agree on a reporting and inventory system that accurately reflects the nation's carbon pollution load. Once we have that number, we have the 2009/2010 baseline against which we will measure our reductions in future years.

Based on these numbers, the government will set a timeline and targets for reducing carbon emissions (and other emissions that contribute to climate change, such as nitrogen) by 90 percent by 2050. Recognizing that it will take some time for industry to respond, we will start with a 20 percent reduction in the aggregate amount of carbon pollution allowed from 2010 to 2020, averaging about 2 percent less per year. From 2020 to 2040 the rate of reduction, again computed against the 2009/2010 baseline, will increase to 3 percent per year. That means we'll reduce 50 percent from the 2009/2010 baseline by 2030, and 80 percent by 2040.

This, by the way, is ten years faster than scientists say is necessary to achieve an 80 percent reduction, because I don't want to avert catastrophe by a matter of seconds. Global-warming emissions reduction isn't a NASCAR race, it's policy, and we can meet our deadlines and targets in an orderly, planned fashion. We should build in this kind of buffer because we can't predict (for instance) whether other countries will act as fast as they should or whether our system will adequately cover unanticipated increases or problems (such as whether efforts to bury carbon permanently underground prove successful).

After establishing the 2009/2010 baseline, the government will set up both an auction of the rights to emit the permitted amount of carbon as well as a system for buyers to trade (buy or sell) their rights as they may decide is necessary.

In 2010, the government would hold its first auction, offering carbon emitters the opportunity to bid against one another for (for instance) a short- or long-term carbon emissions permit. Entities desperate to secure carbon emission rights will buy longer-term permits and will probably pay a higher price. Entities that are gradually reducing their emissions might buy a shorter-term permit at a lower cost. Some might buy a longer-term permit *and* a shorter-term permit to cover the emissions they project over the next five to ten years. Some facilities that emit large amounts of carbon (such as older, less-efficient coal or natural gas electric facilities) will likely be retired or slowed down in the first ten or fifteen years, as their owners explore and develop alternative production methods that don't produce so much carbon. If companies underestimated their need for a permit, they would have to wait for the next auction or purchase rights from a permit owner who decided to make more money by trading the permit than by using her or his pollution right.

Small businesses and emitters would not be included in the early years. Nor would other end users, who take power or natural gas (for instance) from a utility, such as a home or a school. This program would apply to large industrial and utility emitters, or possibly to companies that produce fossil fuels, not to smaller operations that contribute relatively little carbon pollution and that would have difficulty participating in an auction process.

As I say, in a market that reflects and includes costs for carbon, companies that control highly inefficient old electric generating plants, for instance, might decide they can no longer economically justify buying the carbon permits needed to keep an antiquated plant in operation.

They might say to themselves, "You know, we could invest the same amount of money in a new, renewable-energy generating station and actually invest, for profit, the money we would have put into diminishing carbon pollution permits." The return on investment, of course, would have to be attractive.

In today's system, lacking this kind of market-based costing of carbon emission rights, a company that has a choice between projects emitting high amounts at a lower cost and reducing emissions at a higher cost will generally choose the higher-emitting (lower-cost) option. You can't blame them for that. That's like blaming a lion for eating a gazelle—that's what it's programmed to do.

You can't pass a law or hold a protest telling a lion not to eat a gazelle. But if you find a way to attach a cost to environmental destruction, you'll make the ecologically sound project the more profitable choice. The gazelle-hungry lions might turn into emissions-reducing industry leaders. Setting up such goals and systems that protect a broad public interest is an essential function of government.

When companies pay for carbon emission rights at an auction that reflects the permit's true market value, they will think twice about investing in carbon-producing projects or programs.

Together, by auction, the carbon emitters will set the price of carbon. The laws of supply and demand, so integral to market economics, will apply to greenhouse gas emissions. The supply will be limited by regulation (as is, for instance, the nation's monetary supply or the availability of pharmaceuticals, which must be judged safe in a regulatory process before they can be legally marketed), and companies seeking carbon permits will create demand. After they buy the permit, they can trade it, too. There will be a viable market for carbon permits.

This kind of carbon market is called cap and trade. I have likened it to musical chairs for carbon pollution because we would keep pulling away chairs, taking about thirty years to sharply reduce the overall amount of carbon pollution that might be allowed. In the United States, still producing about 25 percent of the world's carbon emissions with just 5 percent of its population, this would mean we need to reduce our emissions—the number of chairs—by 90 percent before 2050. This is similar to the kind of reduction needed in other developed nations in Europe and Asia, although some of these nations have already made reductions for which they will deserve some credit.

Other countries, with large unserved populations and struggling to join the wealthier nations, might actually be allowed to increase emissions because their baseline energy use today is so low. But the preferable way of providing these countries with energy is to pay the small incremental cost of renewable energy and carbon-clean coal, rather than keep using the conventional technologies that spew so much carbon into the atmosphere.

As you will see in chapter 10, where I present my specific proposals for an integrated and comprehensive energy, security, and climate platform, I believe that the developed nations (which will be selling most of that new carbon-clean and renewable technology) can help finance the small incremental cost of doing it right in the developing nations.

In fact, companies in nations where there are requirements to reduce or offset carbon emissions are already investing in new low-carbon energy technologies in other countries. They might buy a wind-generating facility to meet new demand or displace an inefficient old coal plant in a developing nation such as India or China. What is lacking, for now, is the United States' full commitment to making this kind of investment around the world right away. The World Bank, for instance, could be enormously helpful in helping fast-developing nations procure clean-energy technologies and energy efficiency.

China is an interesting example. Here's Peabody Coal again. Peabody is enormously and increasingly involved in China's energy development. The company wants to help develop the electricity that a huge number of new consumers want and deserve. Unfortunately, at this point, the company seems to want to postpone carbon-clean coal development costs as long as it can.

Peabody's preference is for conventional coal technology. The company scoffs at the probability and the risks of climate change. A friend witnessed a presentation by Peabody chairman and CEO Greg Boyce in Utah in spring 2007 at which Boyce showed poll results indicating that Americans would rather see climate change than lose millions of American jobs.

That is a deliberate misrepresentation of cost, made to produce a certain reaction: opposition to needed reforms that will save the global climate.

The truth is, we don't have to lose millions of American jobs when we decide to reduce carbon emissions. In fact, doing it right could *create* millions of new jobs, high-paying jobs in a stable energy sector. If the United States produces, sells, and exports new energy technologies into hungry markets around the world, we could see a huge new wave of growth and investment, one that could dwarf the high-technology boom of the 1990s. Opening new markets to this kind of American technology isn't the only result of this kind of policy. I think General Electric and some other companies really understand that.

We need to hold players like Peabody accountable, not just in the United States but worldwide, and figure out how to keep the company involved and profitable in providing better energy options.

How do we match Peabody's ability to help develop energy resources with the Chinese market? How do we get new technology on the ground, in combination with new options to strip out and geologically dispose of the carbon dioxide that we can separate out during coal gasification?

By answering these questions, we address the larger issues of global climate change. But if the world's governments—especially that of the United States—aren't pushing for carbon-clean options, then there will continue to be a myopic and risky definition of cost. Costs will be defined by the companies that don't want to pay them—as the automobile companies for years have resisted the costs of increased fuel economy. If Japan, China, and Europe can afford those costs—and save their drivers thousands of dollars every year—the United States can figure a way to pay them, as well. European governments deprive themselves of gasoline tax revenues (which are much higher than ours) by encouraging and requiring fuel economy. Yet they know they are doing the right thing for their people and their economies at the same time. A government should act in the interests of its people, not itself.

. . .

We need to be careful about how we use the proceeds of the carbon permit auctions. There are many sensible things we could do with those revenues. I don't believe we should hold them in a large government slush fund for future research or specific technology development. Let the private players in the free market, not the government, make those decisions.

Instead, we can use those auction proceeds to enhance the new energy economy. They can pay for new programs to weatherize low- and middle-income homes. (This is similar to how we dedicated part of New Mexico's windfall oil and natural gas revenues to energy rebates for drivers and households as well as additional weatherization and efficiency investments after prices rose in 2004 and 2005.) They can pay for the rebates that will give car buyers an incentive to purchase plug-in cars. They can fund state and local Climate Challenge grants for innovation and local solutions. In other words, we can leverage that revenue not just into discouraging carbon emissions by creating a price signal and cost, but also into encouraging the right kinds of new energy investment in homes, schools, and businesses. It's a twofer.

We need to expand our investment in new technologies, but the concept of a $10 billion or $15 billion annual research fund or a $50 billion annual carbon tax on corporations that produces a bunch of revenue for a government-directed technology fund is a mistake waiting to happen. First, we take all that money out of the economy, and the government sits on it. Then investors and entrepreneurs need to convince a government-run body to cut loose funding for their projects. Unavoidably, a senator or a representative will say that some of that money should go to this start-up or that campus research facility in their state or district. We might not get a "bridge to nowhere" from this process, but we'll definitely get research projects and investments to nowhere.

No! A thousand times no! How about a private-public investment partnership—run by a mixed board of directors—with the mission of partnering on projects that pay back within ten years and create new funding for further investment? Doesn't that sound a lot better?

It's too costly to have the government collect and allocate the proceeds of some kind of carbon tax. I would much prefer directing carbon auction revenues into specific, known, planned incentives and supports that do the basic work of making energy use more efficient and getting plug-in cars on the road.

Another price of our inaction on energy and climate is what we pay to defend and protect the existing global energy system. It would cost us far less in the long run to recognize that we are paying hidden subsidies into this world energy system and that we are creating future costs in the form of climate change impacts. We are subsidizing a system that could easily end up costing us far more if prices rise because of a storm, a terrorist attack, or rising demand around the world.

A few years ago, before he became defense secretary for President Bush, Robert Gates participated in an exercise to look at the United States' vulnerability to some kind of oil shock. He was quoted as saying, "The real lesson here [is that] it only requires a relatively small amount of oil to be taken out of the system to have huge economic and security implications." The exercise considered geopolitical instability and oil infrastructure vulnerability to terrorist attack. A June 2005 report by Oil Shockwave, the exercise that Gates participated in, points out the "myth of foreign oil: Oil is a fungible commodity that essentially has a single world benchmark price. Therefore, a supply disruption anywhere in the world affects oil consumers everywhere in the world. U.S. exposure to world price shocks is a function of the amount of oil we consume and is not significantly affected by the ratio of 'domestic' to 'imported' product." What that says is that it is meaningless to talk about just reducing our dependence on *foreign* oil. We need to reduce our dependence on *all* oil.

Every moment that we fail as a nation to address this potential oil price shock is a moment wasted and a moment of opportunity for those who wish us ill. In other words, things are bad now because oil prices have risen high (and stayed up) already. But imagine if they were to double or triple. We are providing terrorists and rogue nations with a convenient economic and security target that could deeply affect the United States and help throw the world economy into recession or even depression.

An energy-related international economic crisis can come in many forms beyond oil shocks, though.

Weather disruption and drought, disease and famine—the combined impacts of climate change could "rip apart societies from one side of the planet to the other," providing opportunities for dictators and terrorists to gain control of nations and people around the world. (This is from "Terror in the Weather Forecast: Linking Climate Upheaval and Global Instability," an opinion piece by Thomas Homer-Dixon in the *New York Times*, May 24, 2007.)

Regular industry could also suffer. A recent report on Australia's economically powerful mining industry pointed out that even today, with the drought being experienced in parts of Australia, mining companies have had to cut back on production at key mines ("Australia's Drought Puts Squeeze on Mining," *Wall Street Journal*, May 17, 2007).

And military leaders are concerned about national security and terrorism threats that could result from climate change. Climate disruption will create chaos and dislocation among many of the world's poorest people, contributing both to economic suffering and to alienation against powerful nations (such as the United States) that are perceived to be the largest contributors to climate change. Climate change could force "massive migrations, increased border tensions, greater demands for rescue and evacuation efforts, and conflicts over essential resources, including food and water," said a board of premier military commanders and officers. Such developments could lead to direct U.S. military involvement. Although conservatives objected strongly when Democratic congressional representatives suggested funding to study these impacts, the fact remains that climate change creates untold, unguessed-at openings in the world's and the United States' security.

Who's responsible for high oil prices? Why are Americans paying such a high cost for energy?

It isn't a pretty picture. Just before I wrote this chapter, I read that oil companies and oil-producing nations are fighting over who's responsible for high-priced oil. The companies are defending themselves, saying that refinery glitches in the United States are crimping gasoline supplies. (In fact, they are also now saying they won't expand refinery capacity, long blamed by the oil companies for price spikes in the United States, because we are investing in competitive biofuels that reduce the market for gasoline and diesel fuels.) The oil-producing nations are saying that they don't plan to increase production to ease prices, because the oil companies are making money hand over fist and should cough up profits before the folks who own the reserves would make efforts to increase supplies. It's a convenient little tempest in a teapot. Having jawboned the producers when prices were high in the 1990s (but nowhere near where they are today), I

138

can understand why the Saudis and the Kuwaitis, for instance, would tell the oil-hungry nations to pinch the companies first.

Whoever's to blame, prices are high, profits are in record territory, and oil-producing nations are importing petrodollars at a land-office rate. We can't count on anyone except ourselves to protect our interests. The greatest leverage that Russia and other energy giants can hold over the United States and its allies—and our voice for human rights—is the leverage we give them by growing too dependent on resources that they provide in a world market that doesn't recognize nationalities, boundaries, or national interests. We have created these costs by growing dependent on oil, and necessarily on foreign oil.

Opponents of action on energy and climate ask how I can economically justify my proposals. First, these proposals are necessary to avoid much higher costs if we don't act. Second, the opponents have always exaggerated the costs of new technologies and rules. I think the new requirements might increase costs, but as our experience in New Mexico has shown, wind power looks pretty darn cheap when natural gas prices rise. Last, I am not out to defend the status quo. I know we need to change. By changing, we will create jobs and stabilize our economy. People who decide our energy future based on the price tag have already made too many mistakes. We can't afford to be cheap in the long run.

Overall, there are numerous costs to handling energy policy the way we have been. There are environmental costs, household and business costs, military costs, and national security costs. We can avoid some huge costs that would be associated with climate change by doing the things we need to do to create energy independence. We are already paying price premiums for oil and natural gas. The time has come to invest in our energy future in ways that benefit *us*. The value will be immense.

CHAPTER 7

Government Must Play a Role

Oil prices are very high today, as they have been for the past several years. Part of the problem is that the price of oil has been so unpredictable that investors haven't gotten a steady price signal that it is worth investing in alternatives, or even in efficiency. But part of the problem is also that the administration has had a laissez-faire, hands-off response to high oil prices, despite the damage they are doing to our people and our economy.

In 1998, as I assumed leadership at the Department of Energy, we knew that $10 a barrel was too low. It discouraged new investment in oil and gas development. It caused some operators to curtail basic maintenance or shut in marginally productive wells. When oil was at $10 a barrel, we knew it encouraged profligate behavior that wasted irreplaceable oil. It destabilized international markets. It discouraged people who could have implemented alternatives and efficiency. (It also starved despots and terrorists of needed funding, which wasn't a bad thing, and for a time it weakened the oil cartel's influence over world production.)

In the history of the global oil market, there likely had never been a brief period of such rapid low-to-high fluctuations in oil pricing as during those two or three years when I was secretary, from 1998 to 2001, especially in the absence of a major international embargo or war. Those few years showed how unpredictable world oil markets have become and how dangerous it is for any nation to become overreliant on oil.

Free market advocates—price purists—in economic circles (including some with whom I sparred inside the Clinton administration) said the 2000 price rise was natural and should be allowed to play out. Higher prices, they said, would provide an incentive for more production, and bigger supplies would result in lower prices.

Theoretically speaking, that may have been correct at the time. But that theory ignores the impact on real people, real businesses, and the real U.S. interest in long-term energy independence. It also ignores global warming's impact on the people of the United States and the world. It's a reflexive, almost ideological response. Elected officials should keep people-oriented and longer-term interests, not just the theory of the markets, topmost in their minds.

For the average person, there may be nothing more exasperating than seeing a high government official or an academic economist earnestly defending the workings of the market, explaining how "the most effective way to discourage energy use is to tax it." Those taxes would hurt the economy overall, possibly to the point of recession. Worse, they'd most hurt the most vulnerable. What about rural people who depend on trucking for 70 percent of their goods and who need to get around across long distances? Should they have to move to the city? Sell their land? And what about lower-income people who own homes in the depressed part of an urban area and need to commute across the sprawling metro area to get to jobs that pay not much more than minimum wage—I guess they would have to figure out the four-hour round-trip bus route, because a gas tax would make it too expensive for them to drive. Government should provide more sophisticated, integrated, and compassionate policies. A tax-based carbon policy is one that would change the face and muscle of America. It would definitely widen the gap between the haves and the have-nots. Policy makers and pundits owe the American people better, more effective solutions.

In properly functioning markets, the hardest-working and most innovative companies win, and the weakest lose. The goal of the government is to keep that dynamic going and protect the innocent. But we in government play a role that market players do not: trying to assist with competition and choice, which is anathema to those who dominate any industry. It's why Teddy Roosevelt busted the trusts; it's why we have the Federal Communications Commission to oversee the use of our airwaves; and it's why we regulate weights and measures at gasoline pumps. People in the industry don't necessarily like it, but it's necessary.

When oil prices rose to what seemed unimaginable heights in 2000, I thought there was a further role for government. Prices were hurting people and businesses, even though the energy intensity of our economy had been reduced over the previous two decades. As energy secretary, I felt that it was my duty to act, to try to bring prices back into a safe and stable range while also pressing for development of alternatives that would help wean us off oil. Just as important, I focused on making sure the federal government took steps to protect those in our society who were most vulnerable to oil price increases, such as people in the Northeast who use oil to heat their homes. To me, the price of inaction would be too high.

I had four areas where I could take the initiative: talk to OPEC, encourage more oil production, use the U.S. Strategic Petroleum Reserve, and assist the hardest-hit Americans.

It was critical for the U.S. energy secretary to show oil producers around the world that we were not going to sit idly by and accept sharp oil price increases. The Saudis, for instance, weren't totally pleased when I embarked on what some people called a "jawboning" mission to seek Saudi and OPEC production increases that could help mitigate the sudden price spikes.

Jawboning isn't military; it isn't regulatory; it isn't strategic. It's a tactic we use to change perception—to focus world or national attention, to create bad publicity or a sense of obligation, and to begin signaling that we are concerned and starting to take action. There is a delicate balance on a jawboning mission.

First, the world's economic leader and most dominant force could hardly be seen to come hat in hand, tin cup extended, looking for handouts or concessions. The United States must never be subservient or obsequious, and must assure that it protects its own interests. Yet the Saudis and others knew that they had us over a barrel (an oil barrel, of course). The ownership of large oil reserves builds that type of self-confidence.

When I went to meet with Saudi king Fahd, he kept me waiting in a small waiting room. A half hour, an hour, two hours passed. Obviously I could tell what was going on. Hours later, after a good conversation with the king, I took my staff out on a shopping trip, making us very late for a state dinner. That was my way of saying that I must have left my tin cup at home. The message got through, and from then on our appointments and communications with the Saudis were more respectful and punctual.

The Saudis were keenly aware that they were being asked to produce more oil, quickly, to prop up a U.S. oil economy that they regarded as profligate and undisciplined. (You can't miss the irony here. Gulf nations generally share a propensity for state-subsidized oil sales at low prices to their own citizens, as well as for big gas-guzzling cars and energy-intensive business and tourism development. Changes in the way oil-owning nations conduct internal energy policy—low prices, subsidies—could have a huge impact not only on energy use and climate but also on world markets. If efficiency is an energy resource, as many rightly contend, efficiency measures could produce the equivalent of a gusher's worth of oil a day in these countries.)

In 1985, the Reagan administration had responded to pressure from Detroit automakers and actually rolled back fuel economy standards for a few years, until Congress acted to restore them. By the mid-1990s, the combined fuel economy of our auto and light truck fleets was basically stalled. Despite Vice President Gore's and President Clinton's strong commitment to fuel economy and energy efficiency, the combination of GOP control of the House of Representatives and the concern of Democrats from automobile states like Michigan was a seemingly permanent obstacle to increased fuel economy in American markets—very different from Europe and Japan, where there was a commitment to making cars more efficient and to improving public transportation in and between major cities.

The Saudis saw this as a general disdain for conservation. The United States had indeed failed to take basic steps that it should have taken to address conservation and efficiency. But I couldn't sit there and participate in self-flagellation or, worse, what could be perceived as an external verbal attack on the

United States. I had to figure out how to call for more efficiency and conservation in my final communiqué with the Saudi oil minister without appearing to sell out previous administrations and the current Congress, which had opposed fuel efficiency improvements and technological change. Even though we strongly disagreed with those efficiency opponents, foreign policy needs to be consistent and other nations need to see a *united* United States. Thus, we included a commitment to conservation and efficiency efforts in our final communiqué—a commitment that would have helped reduce our nation's exposure to the very much higher oil prices that hit and stuck in 2003–2004, had the George W. Bush administration followed up on it.

One of the ways our nation could have started on a better energy track was to pursue the high-mileage initiative I worked on at the Department of Energy, aimed at getting an 80-mile-per-gallon car onto the market. Unfortunately, that initiative was cast aside when the new administration came into office. Further, possibly out of a reflex against a previous Democratic administration rather than out of policy interest, the new administration has refused to jawbone on oil prices, saying that it prefers private dialogue with oil producers.

My view is that jawboning can't really be effective *unless* it's public. Private jawboning—if it has even occurred during the most recent and sustained price run-up—is a contradiction in terms and has likely had little effect. The price of oil is about triple what it was when the Bush administration took office. If they jawboned, it certainly doesn't show in the prices Americans are paying at the pump.

My jawboning effort, disparaged by political opponents, was successful, in combination with my other efforts. Oil prices settled back down by the end of 2000, as the Clinton administration was leaving office. Our actions to secure Northeast heating oil supplies in the late summer had paid off, and the price increases were not nearly as damaging as we had feared.

Our release of oil from the Strategic Petroleum Reserve (SPR)—it's called "strategic" for a reason—helped dampen prices here in the United States and showed the world market players that we were willing to take aggressive, competitive countermeasures to address high prices. (The United States actually made money in the process, according to my understanding from former Department of Energy staff. We sold oil out of the SPR when prices were very high and later restocked the same amount at a lower price as oil markets settled down.)

Over the past five years the Bush administration has refused to use the SPR to wage war on high prices, much as it dropped our high-efficiency auto program. In fact, it built the reserve up by buying oil at high prices, the opposite of our approach when I was energy secretary. Oil prices are a function of many factors, of course, and the Bush administration's failure to jawbone, failure to pursue fuel-efficient automobiles in the Department of Energy, and failure to use the SPR as a market tool aren't necessarily the reason that Americans are facing record-high gasoline prices now (and have been facing them for several years). But from its earliest days, the Bush administration closed the oil-price-fighting toolbox and definitely sent a hands-off signal into the world oil marketplace.

Theories about oil prices are fine. In the case of the Bush administration, however, theory turned into ideology and partisanship. The federal government simply withdrew from areas it should have been involved in. A few years after taking office, when oil prices rose, President Bush himself seemed to recognize the error of the administration's ideology, stating his concern about our "addiction to oil" in his State of the Union addresses, and calling for an annual 4 percent increase in fuel economy standards even though the administration had tossed out fuel efficiency technology programs only a few years earlier. It has been an erratic performance, one that has resulted in the highest sustained gasoline and oil prices ever.

The federal government can play a huge, constructive role in supporting diverse and competitive energy markets and technologies. If it chooses the course of inaction, as we have seen, there is a price paid by people and businesses across the country. The leaders of the federal government should always remember that high energy prices have genuine, hard-hitting impacts on people and businesses. It's our job to try to reduce those impacts by market mechanisms such as supporting competition and new technologies—aspects of energy policy that have been outrageously undercut by the policies of the Bush administration, despite the interests of every American (Republican, Democrat, or other) in competitive, diverse energy markets.

Most people around the United States don't know about the extreme poverty and disillusionment on the huge Navajo reservation that spreads across northwest New Mexico and northeast Arizona. This desolate, craggy, arid landscape is home to more than 200,000 people, many of whom speak neither English nor Spanish, only their native tongue.

My first major achievement as a congressman, with most of the Navajo Nation in my district, was securing desperately needed funding for a community project that had languished for years. I wanted this as my first accomplishment, not just to show Navajo voters that their congressional representative cared about their needs and their future, but perhaps to create more optimism and commitment to voting among the Navajo people.

Sentient Americans understand the injustices Native Americans have experienced and how important their contributions have been to making America a great nation. The patriotism of the Navajo people is shown all over the Navajo Nation, in flags and bumper stickers, despite the bad hand their people were dealt. Navajo soldiers have fought (like other Native Americans) in our foreign wars, and the Navajo code talkers played a great role in ending World War II—a story worth studying if you have never heard about it.

I have been welcomed into Navajo homes that have no electricity and sit dozens of miles from the nearest telephone or electric pole. I have eaten the native foods and joined in the traditional ceremonies. I now have many friends in this mostly forgotten but sovereign land, and I will do almost anything to support them.

So when I campaigned to be elected New Mexico governor in 2002, one of the first things I heard about from my Navajo friends was a long-standing concern. Since the 1920s, when the first major highway was built across Navajo land, it has been an issue. For some misbegotten and insulting reason, the planners who first built that major highway had numbered it 666.

Of course, many people know that 666 is associated with the devil. Many Navajos, whether Christian or not, are highly spiritual. To have their main route to big cities and other states numbered 666 was like a slap in the face by the highway department, as well as a spiritual jeopardy for a people whose culture had already been severely undercut.

I pledged to renumber that highway as soon as I was elected governor. It wasn't a decision requiring legislative approval. I could make that decision in consultation with the state transportation secretary (an appointee in my cabinet) and the State

Highway Commission (also my appointees). It was, in fact, disgraceful that previous governors and highway administrators had ignored the Navajos' pleas to change that highway number decade after decade.

On the day I took office I put this issue on the list for my staff to accomplish. We started working with the federal highway officials and with Colorado transportation agencies to make sure they knew we were going to change that highway's number. Needless to say, I wouldn't take no for an answer.

The fact that the federal government would have to make changes in its centralized systems didn't bother me. The complaints of some state and federal agency staff about extra legwork and paperwork didn't bother me. We kept moving forward on this change—so insignificant in the world of Washington, where billions of dollars flow into highway programs every day, yet so significant to the Navajo people. And we didn't move forward at the usual glacial pace of government. We pushed hard. I think my reputation among federal agencies, from my years as a congressman and a Cabinet member, probably helped convince federal agency staff that I usually get what I want, and fast.

A few months after I had taken office, a large delegation of Navajo officials and citizens joined me and my transportation secretary, Rhonda Faught, as we pulled a cloth off the new highway sign. Highway 666 had become Highway 491. (Transportation officials who have to justify these things presented a rationale for the new number and how it fit better within the federal system. I was pleased that they had decided the new number worked for them, but what number they selected instead of 666 didn't really matter.)

As we flew back to Santa Fe, a high-calorie Navajo lunch digesting in our stomachs, one of my staff people commented on the tears he had seen in many people's eyes.

This, I explained, is what public office is about. Doing things for people; taking action; making government respond. I, too, was moved and proud to have helped take this monkey off the Navajo Nation's back. I had felt the relief and joy, and I had seen the tears. It was a small but significant victory in government of the people, for the people, and by the people.

On the other hand, I also know there are principles you simply can not violate for political reasons. Government should be led by people who stick to their principles.

Even though I have a long kinship with the Navajo Nation, including committing significant state and federal funding for their needs over the years, I can't do everything they want.

That's also what public office is about. You need to stand up for the principles you represent to the public when you are campaigning and speaking out.

So in 2006, when I learned that the Navajo Nation had negotiated a deal with a big international company (Sithe Global Energy) to put in a coal generating plant in northwest New Mexico, I had several threshold, principle-level issues that I needed to know more about.

First, I knew that the company involved had gotten large tax reductions from the Navajo Nation. I wanted to be sure that further tax incentives from the state would really be necessary. I never was convinced of this. The project was in the billions of dollars, and it seemed that the state's decision about whether to provide funding would be inconsequential compared to whether or not the company could sell the power it would produce. No major utility had come forward to purchase the power. I wondered whether the state would basically end up underwriting a white elephant.

Second, I wanted to be sure that the project would indeed create good jobs for local people. I hoped that the unions would get a share, and I hoped there would be plenty of Navajo representation. This issue languished. My labor liaison kept telling me he had told the company who to call in the labor movement to make sure that New Mexicans and Navajos would truly benefit from the project. It was only in October, a few months before the 2007 New Mexico legislature would convene, that there was some kind of agreement that satisfied the labor community. That issue seemed to have been resolved.

And third, I wanted to be sure that this plant, over which the state would have no permitting authority (because it sits on sovereign Navajo land, where the Navajo Nation and the U.S. Environmental Protection Agency have full jurisdiction), would not make it impossible for New Mexico to sharply reduce its global warming emissions. On this matter, I was not satisfied. The plant was designed to use conventional combustion technologies rather than gasification processes that make it far easier to capture potential greenhouse gas emissions. Despite our inquiries about the possibility of using gasification, the project proponents said the plant was too far along—it couldn't be redesigned to capture carbon emissions, as I believed was necessary.

The Navajo Nation president, Joe Shirley, who is an ally and a friend, supported the project. I also heard from many local Navajos, including some chapters of the Navajo government, who were strongly opposed to the coal plant. When the 2007 legislature started its sixty-day session in Santa Fe just after Martin Luther King Day, I learned that the coal plant's proponents had started lobbying for an $85 million state tax break.

I thought, "That kind of subsidy would dwarf almost any other tax break for an economic development project in New Mexico. It would mean that our largest single investment in an energy project would be for conventional coal without carbon capture. Yet my opposition would be a crushing blow to the Navajo leadership supporting this project."

Let me tell you, there may be no place in the United States as desperate for quality jobs as our Indian reservations. The poverty of the Deep South, blighted urban areas, or Katrina-ravaged New Orleans may be similar, but at least there are jobs within miles of these devastated areas. Not so in Navajo country. A project like this one, known as Desert Rock, was the kind of project that might come around once a century, if that often.

But I struggled with supporting a huge subsidy for Desert Rock. I had pushed through a number of strong new incentives for renewable energy in New Mexico, from elimination of the sales tax on hybrid automobiles to generous tax credits for the installation of solar energy for hot water and electricity, but these totaled in the tens of millions of dollars statewide. To put $85 million into a conventional coal plant would be a huge step in the other direction.

So as the legislative session proceeded, I let it be known—in a way that I hoped would not insult my Navajo friends—that the proposal put forward by Sithe Global Energy for the Desert Rock facility didn't have my automatic support. (By the way, I learned later that Sithe was represented by Bracewell and Giuliani, a well-known energy law firm out of Houston whose principals include GOP presidential candidate Rudy Giuliani. I respect Rudy and am sorry for him that he had such a disappointing introduction to New Mexico, where we try to work with industry to achieve the right results, but we don't really want to get pushed around by big investors who say "My way, plus a big subsidy, or we won't play." On the Desert Rock matter, as with others, we stand by our principles, and we make results, not promises.)

It didn't matter whether the company might try to put the tax subsidy into another bill that they thought I would have to sign. It didn't matter that they tried to make opponents look bad for "killing jobs." I had tried to work with the company on a proposal, such as gasification, that would be acceptable, and they had rejected it. Then they had come in asking for a gigantic subsidy from New Mexico taxpayers. That might be how they do it in Houston or New York, but not here in New Mexico. So the proposed coal plant subsidy died, at least for a year.

I know the U.S. Environmental Protection Agency is going to try to grant Desert Rock a permit before the current administration leaves office. They have made it one of their highest priorities, fast-tracking everything in the permitting process and calling it the cleanest coal plant project in the country.

The EPA's credibility on this kind of issue is substantially less than it used to be under my friend Carol Browner in the Clinton administration. In its comments about Desert Rock, the EPA ignored climate impacts from carbon emissions, failed to ask for investigation of alternative technologies such as gasification, and minimized the potential toxic effect of mercury emissions by making them sound negligible. I have instructed our Environmental Department to oppose them.

Can you believe that the U.S. Environmental Protection Agency doesn't even think about greenhouse gas emissions when it grants a permit for a new coal plant? Neither could the U.S. Supreme Court, which subsequent to our legislative session rejected the EPA's claims that it had no authority or responsibility to regulate carbon emissions under the Clean Air Act.

The EPA's posture violated every single word of that law's title: "Clean," "Air," and "Act."

I had issued an executive order setting aggressive targets for greenhouse gas reductions in New Mexico only two years before.

156

For some reason, the EPA and Sithe believed those targets were meaningless. I guess they figured the politics of the proposal were so strong, and the Navajos were such close friends, that I would stay out of it.

They were wrong. I don't adopt these greenhouse gas targets, set out specific strategies for reducing emissions, tell the world that New Mexico is the Clean Energy State, and urge the Western Governors' Association (successfully, to the surprise of many) to adopt my policy resolution to "slow, stop, and reverse" greenhouse gas emissions only to turn around and make a special deal for a project based on politics.

Elected officials should use politics to enact good policies, not enact policies because they make good politics. I want to work with the Navajo Nation on more positive alternatives.

I am not a great candidate for extortion, which Sithe would probably have known if they had spent more time in New Mexico. Several years ago I accepted an offer from the Los Alamos National Laboratory (LANL) to lend me a few staff people to help in the governor's office, in particular with science and economic development. It was the kind of arrangement that could benefit both sides—unless it got political or the LANL staffers followed their own agenda instead of the one I am carrying out for New Mexico. I was fairly satisfied with the arrangement for the first year or two.

Then one day an LANL official stopped by my office. He said that LANL was disappointed with my administration's hard-fought battle to win environmental cleanup at LANL. He said what we wanted was expensive and unreasonable. When he didn't get what he wanted, he said that LANL would have to take back one of the four staff people they had delegated to work in my office.

It was about two o'clock in the afternoon. By five o'clock they were all gone—the LANL official *and* the four delegated staffers. LANL rolled a cherry bomb into my office without knowing that there was a howitzer behind the door.

One of my own advisors—not from LANL—told me that the LANL staffers were not surprised. They were actually sort of embarrassed by the amateurish effort at extortion coming from the top at LANL. I have kept working with most of them individually on special projects—even though they had to clean out their offices and disappear in just three hours.

("You're fired" is one of my favorite spoofy joke lines with my staff and even with people I hardly know, like a Utah state trooper who thought I was serious when I kept saying it to him on a trip to Salt Lake City two years ago. A couple of years ago, when *Newsweek* ran a story about Donald Trump's television show *The Apprentice*, the cover showed a large picture of The Donald's head, with YOU'RE FIRED in large print. Ned Farquhar, my energy staffer, gave me a memo congratulating me for making the cover of *Newsweek*—"See attached," he said. When I turned the page I saw the picture of my head pasted over Trump's and realized it was a joke. But there it was—my favorite joke phrase: "You're fired!" I read Ned's memo in my pile of homework during a Cabinet meeting, and I had trouble suppressing a laugh. I sent it on to my wife, Barbara, hoping it would have the same effect on her.)

Going back to the Sithe and Desert Rock episodes and my earlier story about Peabody's proposal for the Mustang coal plant, this was the second major coal plant that my administration had stood up to. In both cases I offered help and incentives to develop a carbon-clean facility, and the industry rejected them.

I am a good friend of coal miners. I see the coal industry as

integral to our economic future. Many of my governor friends—
such as West Virginia's Joe Manchin, Rod Blagojevich of Illinois,
and Ed Rendell of Pennsylvania, whom I know very well from
chairing the strong and growing Democratic Governors' Association for a couple of terms—are coal advocates. I work closely
with them. I hope they will succeed at putting in place the right
kind of incentives so that coal can generate truly clean, competitive power that doesn't threaten our climate.

That's one reason I pushed for an advanced energy incentives bill in the New Mexico legislature at the same time I was
showing concern about Desert Rock. If Sithe didn't want to
come forward with a carbon-clean coal proposal, I wanted to
show the rest of the coal industry that I was willing to put New
Mexico money on the table to provide incentives for the right
kinds of energy development, including coal.

I remember a Western Governors' Association public meeting in Washington several years ago when my friend Dave
Freudenthal from Wyoming sat down during an energy session,
looked across the horseshoe table, and apropos of pretty much
nothing asked, "Richardson, have you learned to say 'coal' yet?"
Unfortunately, the coal industry, powerful in Wyoming,
has tried to define me as being completely against coal. New
Mexico's new advanced energy incentives show that this is
wrong. I think Dave now realizes how important it is to move to
new technologies to protect the climate. I hear he might even
start up a climate change task force in Wyoming—something
that certainly would never occur in Wyoming without gubernatorial leadership, inspired by clean-energy progress across the
West. We need solar, we need wind, and sometimes we need
carbon-clean coal.

Under New Mexico's new law, a large coal or solar project
meeting at least the same carbon emissions profile as natural

gas—about 60 percent less than conventional coal—can get a tax credit in the range of $60 million, so a coal gasification plant would qualify. It has been my hope to attract investors who will want to develop solar and advanced coal. I have talked with coal companies, utilities, and private investors all over the country about this concept.

We couldn't use that much power in New Mexico even if it were clean. In the whole state we use only about 4,500 megawatts. So this is New Mexico stepping out ahead of other states and saying, "We want clean power in the West. We want to help industry start reducing its greenhouse gas emissions. We want the large metro-area markets—from Phoenix and Denver and Salt Lake City all the way out to Las Vegas, San Diego, L.A., and San Francisco—to buy really clean power from New Mexico. We want clean-energy jobs for our people."

Further, a coal gasification project would be a good balance to encourage the development of New Mexico's plentiful wind energy. We have from 6,000 to 12,000 megawatts of excellent wind potential sitting on the seam of three electric grids—the Western grid, the Southwest grid, and the Texas grid. Using natural gas or coal-based gas to power turbines also offers another advantage over conventional coal combustion. Gas turbines can be adjusted or turned on and off faster than a large coal burner. So they work better in combination with wind energy (which can come on and offline very suddenly) and help keep transmission lines full. "Shaping" conventional power to intermittent renewable energy supplies should be a goal when we consider energy alternatives.

With that much wind, I have also instituted incentives for wind development that would serve other states, since our own demand can't use all we have, much as in the Dakotas or Wyoming, where the wind is so plentiful and the people so few.

For instance, I worked for three years to get our legislature to create a Renewable Energy Transmission Authority whose purpose is to help clear transmission paths for all that wind and sun in New Mexico, getting the energy across state borders. It will benefit the ranchers where most of that wind and sun is found (who happen to be mostly Republicans, and who still vote for me—I won thirty-two of thirty-three New Mexico counties in the last election), it will benefit our state revenues, and it will benefit the markets where it is sold—Arizona or Utah or Nevada, potentially even California.

And because we have instituted extensive mine safety and environmental safeguards for coal mining in New Mexico, I believe we can conduct mining operations relatively safely. Any energy production is going to entail some environmental risk and damage, from birds and bats that might be killed by giant wind turbines in their night migration patterns to the habitat destruction that can accompany a huge solar installation. We need to choose options that balance out best for affordability, minimum environmental damage, worker safety, water supplies, and climate impact.

The point of this story is that I made strong commitments on greenhouse gas controls, and, despite the destructive policies of our nation's Environmental Protection Agency, I stood up for those commitments regardless of the politics inside New Mexico. Then I went a step further. I proposed acceptable solutions to the company interested in building a major coal plant and got a law into place cementing an incentive program at the same time I was concerned about the giant tax subsidy the company wanted for conventional technology. I like taking constructive action, and that's what I did.

My staff and people from conservation organizations around the country believe that the tax subsidy for Desert Rock would have passed without my administration's opposition. (It will probably be proposed again in the 2008 legislature, I hear.) They say Desert Rock was the biggest single lobbying force in the 2007 legislature.

I credit the Navajo leadership for never threatening me by saying they wouldn't work with me again or that they would try to hurt me at the ballot box. We remain close friends even if I can't do everything they want. They understand principle.

The coal community should know that I am willing to help them do it right. The world is changing, and they can act as U.S. automakers have acted over recent decades—sacrificing jobs and market share by crying out that every change in the fuel economy standards will put them out of business—or they can work constructively to build a positive future for coal that is cleaner and cleaner and cleaner. I choose the latter, more sensible pathway to energy production, protecting our national interest and the climate, and working together to create good long-term jobs for people who need them. As I say, government must play a role in the nation's energy choices and its energy future.

CHAPTER 8

Using the Bully Pulpit: The Power of the Energy President

M y years at the head of the U.S. Department of Energy were anything but unchallenging. They were trial by fire. I learned a huge amount that would be useful in the White House, where I intend to make energy and climate policy a central priority.

As noted on pages 60–61, I was energy secretary when the recently deregulated California power system began to unravel in 2000. We subsequently learned of the large role that Enron and other energy providers played in the process, gaming the electricity markets in our most populated state.

Some people called it the California energy crisis. It could have been called the California energy disaster.

During the California energy crisis, spot market prices for electricity suddenly rose to levels more than a hundred times as high as they had previously been. Because California's recent deregulation law prevented most long-term electricity contracts (in hopes that generators would compete to drive prices down over the long term), public and private utilities were in a very difficult position—buy high in the spot market or cut consumption. In addition, reduced supplies of electricity threatened blackouts and brownouts on what seemed like a daily basis.

Like a California surfer (and I use this simile satirically, which I need to say because so many critics want to corner or dirty presidential candidates out of context), I saw this wave coming before it broke. I was already concerned about electricity reliability on the West Coast—whether the supply of electricity would meet the demand and whether the electric transmission system and the markets were set to function correctly. In the spring of 2000 I headed out to California to hold a reliability summit side-by-side with California utility representatives, state officials, and consumer advocates. I heard rumors that others thought this activist approach was risky—that we could look as if *we* owned the reliability problem when supplies eventually shortened, and that people would blame us for not doing enough to prevent it.

Avoiding a problem, however, has never been my forte.

Instead of a pleasant rolling breaker, this wave crashed on California like the perfect storm.

First, natural gas prices rose suddenly across the United States. Electricity prices rose in a lot of places where natural gas is important to electric supply. California has air pollution problems and local opposition to building most types of new power plants. So it had grown increasingly dependent on natural gas generation in recent decades, because natural gas burns relatively cleanly and its generation infrastructure can be built quickly.

Second, the economy was very strong, pushing up the demand for electricity. The high-tech sector had carried the U.S. economy to new heights, with a particularly significant boost to California's economy. In the 1990s, as Asia began to emerge from weak economic conditions, no place was more involved in new Asia-America trade than California. California is right there on the Pacific Rim, within relatively short distance of technology-hungry Asia. Its economy was bustling.

Third, it was a hot and dry summer in California and on the rest of the West Coast. In most of the state, air conditioning went on, creating sharp spikes in demand—a real opportunity for manipulators to close down a few peak generating facilities and force the utilities and the California transmission authorities to scour other states looking for electricity. To the north, growing markets and a drought limited the availability of hydropower from Washington and Oregon, which traditionally export energy to California in the summer.

I, and others, called for conservation. California has always prided itself, rightly, on its conservation policies. But there was much more that could be done, as was shown during the months of the California electricity crisis. People and businesses, acting in the public interest as well as to save themselves money, cut their electricity use by as much as 10 percent at times. This critical reduction helped prevent peak power purchases that would have cost hundreds and hundreds of millions of dollars.

I was on the phone just about every day with authorities at the California Independent System Operator (Cal ISO). These are the people who anticipate overall demand on a day-to-day basis and figure out how to make sure the grid is carrying adequate electricity to meet projected demand in the complicated mosaic of private utilities, municipal utilities, and member-controlled cooperatives that make up the California electric market.

167

I knew—and they knew—that we were facing a major challenge, one that could change the West's economic destiny and severely affect people's lives. It was important for the federal energy secretary to take the reins, coordinate people, and anticipate and resolve problems.

I know I aggravated relations even with some of my Democratic allies in government in California, Oregon, and Washington when I ordered two federal utilities—the Bonneville Power Administration and the Western Area Power Administration—to export more hydropower generated at federal dams in the West. I kept pushing local and state authorities right until the end of my tenure as energy secretary. Even in January 2001, when the Bush administration was about to take office, I called a California energy summit, invited various powerful people—from Treasury Secretary Larry Summers to economic advisor Gene Sperling, California governor Gray Davis, Senator Dianne Feinstein of California, even Enron's Ken Lay—and laid out plans for continuing to address the crisis. We followed up with a further action-planning meeting a week later, although the president sent me to Saudi Arabia to deal with oil issues and I couldn't participate.

Overall, I was surprised by the economists' general view that the market should be allowed to perform and correct itself, despite the supposedly short-term pain of excruciatingly high prices. Sure, in the long run it could all work out. But as the revered economist John Maynard Keynes famously said, in the long run we'll all be dead.

Senator Feinstein was hands-on and involved. She wanted to solve the problem. She saw the federal government's role and was a real activist. I developed even greater respect for her through this painful process. I was also impressed by the professional people at Cal ISO in particular. They were a sophisticated group, technically knowledgeable, practical, committed to hard work. They hinted that they thought there might be market manipulation occurring, but there was no real proof until after I had left office. No one would have known better, and their acumen helped expose the market manipulation by Enron and other traders within months.

During the California energy crisis, I was reminded how bad advice and bad staff work can hurt elected officials. Voters choose us for who we are, not for who advises us or their advice. It boils down to our own decisions, our own judgments, our own connection with the voters. We need to be comfortable with and support the people who work closely with us, but we can't depend on them. That's one of the great challenges of holding public office—we're the elected ones, we see and talk with voters, yet so much of what happens depends on staff. I am not sure California's then governor Gray Davis got everything he could have from his staff, or understood the staff's role the way I do.

At one point in our strategy and negotiating sessions related to California's desperate electricity, Treasury Secretary Summers and I held a work session that went pretty much all night. We called in California officials, staff, industry people, and agency experts. Late at night one of Governor Davis's staffers approached me and asked to end the session, saying the governor needed to get to bed. He was tired. I exploded. I wanted the governor there, and I wanted him and his staff to recognize the opportunity we had to solve issues, with everybody in one place. No, we don't need to work all night every night, but when the people of California were facing a very difficult situation, an expensive one that could fundamentally affect its people and its economy, I thought it was worth working hard through the clock.

By rushing him away and keeping their distance from the problem solving, Governor Davis's advisors had prevented his playing a central role in confronting a crisis of major proportions. That's a situation I won't ever be in. What was interesting was that we continued the meeting. We kept working. I don't always do it perfectly, but I want to be in there making a difference and giving it everything I have.

One day, as I was working with Senator Feinstein, Governor Davis, and the chairman of the Federal Energy Regulatory Commission, I received a call from Cal ISO notifying me that electricity suppliers and utilities outside California were threatening to withhold sales of power into California because they were worried that they were not going to get paid back, since two of California's major utilities were near bankruptcy. I explored my authority as energy secretary, looking for ways I could help. I invoked statutory powers, which had never been previously used by an energy secretary, to force utilities and other electricity generators to sell power into the marketplace.

Nobody was happy about it—except for millions of anonymous Californians whose refrigerators and lights stayed on—but I had that authority and I used it. It required me to issue new orders regularly, and I kept doing it weekly, as I recall. The power kept flowing into California, frustrating the as-yet-unexposed ambitions and hopes of those energy traders who were trying to manipulate the market. In fact, it was later revealed—in the transcribed Enron traders' phone conversation that I quoted back in chapter 3—that the energy traders were eager for me to leave office so that they could get back to manipulating the market.

One of the exciting political issues during the California energy crisis was that the Democratic presidential nominating convention was in Los Angeles during that summer of rolling blackouts. Needless to say, there was some nervousness around the White House, and particularly the vice president's office, that it would be a bad thing if the lights and sound went out, leaving

170

tens of thousands of screaming Democrats clustered in a dark, hot arena. The very thought was chilling, like extreme air conditioning—or a sauna, take your pick—for an energy secretary. I think I talked to the people at Cal ISO every few minutes throughout the convention, and my friend Al Gore cakewalked to a resounding nomination.

We can't know what kind of Enron-like market manipulation affects world oil markets. We *do* know that more than 80 percent of the world's oil reserves are controlled by nationalized oil companies. We also know that there are fewer and fewer multinational oil companies trading oil and developing it. Further, we know that a single cartel, OPEC, has the power to affect production and at least influence the price of oil. In other words, even though there may be things happening behind the scenes that we don't know about, it is clear from just the things we do know that we are unwise to be overly dependent on a commodity such as oil, whose price is out of our control, whose supply is largely controlled by cartels and national oil companies, and whose market is dominated by a very small core of very powerful oil companies. We don't know for sure, but even a rock-ribbed conservative such as Bill O'Reilly of Fox News says, "It isn't capitalism. It's a fixed market [for oil]" (May 25, 2007, Monterey Institute event on energy policy, broadcast a few days later on C-SPAN).

These companies have done a marvelous job of building a very efficient world trading system for oil. They have had their profitable times, and times when they have lost huge amounts of money. I am not accusing them of market manipulation by including them in this discussion, but I do want to put them on notice: a major component of my energy policy, should I gain the

White House, will be to create competition so that Americans have choices about how to get around and which energy sources they will rely on.

What I mean by "competition" and "choice" is that we should have the plug-in car out there on the roads, quickly. You'll read it elsewhere in this book: I think it is critical for us to help electric cars into the marketplace because they give the consumer a new, sensible choice. He or she could fuel up at a few bucks per hundred miles, instead of paying fifteen to twenty dollars for a hundred miles' worth of gasoline. This kind of competition is now completely lacking in a transportation market that relies on oil for 97 percent of its fuel.

The president and the government have enormous power to change this—far more than an energy secretary or Congress. The president can lay out the vision, the benefits, the conveniences (charge up instead of fill up and tune up) of the plug-in car. He (or she) can ask the country to consider this plug-in car option, and ride in one himself. The president can hold a White House summit on low- and no-petroleum vehicles within thirty days of taking office and ask automakers, labor, utilities, and scientists to show how we can achieve aggressive plug-in car targets (not a plan, but an actual policy program).

In the United States, only the president (and perhaps a great and trusted leader like the late Martin Luther King) really has the bully pulpit. I plan to use that bully pulpit for the purpose of uniting Americans behind programs like the plug-in car that are essential to reducing our dependence on oil. Unlike the current residents of the White House, I won't set small goals, I won't prefer oil and gas production, and I won't scoff at or undermine efforts to address climate change. I will jawbone automakers, labor, members of Congress. I know how it's done. I know many of the players very well. I expect results.

. . .

Examples like the California energy crisis and Enron show the need for government oversight and action. As a market-oriented policymaker, I believe that the best approach is for government to set conditions and let the private sector compete for business.

Adam Smith, the Scottish philosopher usually considered the father of free-market economics, published his master work, *The Wealth of Nations*, in the very same year as the American Revolution. He described an "invisible hand" of self-interest that guides commerce and investment. In general, Smith was right. Most financial transactions, and most trade, will build society and create wealth.

However, when common interests, such as the atmosphere, clean water, or public health, are at stake, there must be rules and standards. Thus, as a society we have chosen to regulate everything from land use—using zoning to protect a property owner from the sudden appearance of a dangerous or noxious land use appearing next door—to safety belts, which save tens of thousands of lives every year, reducing society's costs as well as the social impact that those deaths would have caused.

This is certainly how we operate our economy across many levels. For example, a government body—the Federal Reserve—regulates money supply and key interest rates. The decision to manage the economy through the Federal Reserve has allowed our nation to develop by far the world's most robust economy and to adjust to economic ups and downs in ways that have most certainly prevented another Great Depression over the past seventy-five years. Our nation has learned to regulate its economy but also to allow every imaginable type of investment within it.

Similarly, we regulate what foods and medicines are allowed in the U.S. marketplace through the Food and Drug Administration. This is not to force people into using certain types of food, but to make certain that the choices available to them are safe and won't threaten public health through the spread of botulism or bacteria, for instance. Health inspectors look at our restaurants and our slaughterhouses to protect the public's health. Who has the time or the expertise to do this on her or his own? We need to pool our resources and assign this task to government.

We might have the greatest free market in the world, but we are increasingly sensible and practical about the basic rules we apply to everyone who operates in that free market. It's time for us to learn how to use and improve existing energy markets to encourage the development of new energy resources and alternative technologies, as well as to limit our economy's impact on the global atmosphere.

Why? First, because our individual interests in energy use have misserved the national interest in energy independence.

In 1979, we imported less than 30 percent of our oil. Today we import about 65 percent—which also happens to be the percentage of our oil use dedicated to transportation. About 45 percent of our daily oil use is in gasoline, mostly for single-family trucks and cars. In other words, our individual decisions in the existing marketplace (in which choices are exceedingly constrained by the products the oil trade and auto companies put in the market) are creating and reinforcing our dependence on other nations for energy supplies. As a result, the United States is beholden to other countries that supply our oil. Further, we are heavily involved, having the world's largest open-ocean, blue-water navy, in defending oceanic oil transportation routes and allies such as Saudi Arabia that control and ship oil. The oil companies that move oil around get a large benefit, unpaid for, when we do that. The time has come to figure out how to include these costs, these hidden subsidies paid by U.S. taxpayers, in the cost of oil. This must be done gradually and carefully in cooperation with other nations and in ways that don't disrupt markets.

Second, we need to intervene in the energy markets because the types of energy we have become most reliant on are also the most damaging to the atmosphere.

Carbon dioxide, the major greenhouse gas, exists in nature, and its atmospheric concentrations rise and fall over centuries and millennia. Plants breathe carbon dioxide, and they store carbon, recycling it throughout the atmosphere. The change, which has exponentially increased in the past century and even the past few decades, is that the energy types we rely on today release a lot of *fossil* carbon into the atmosphere. In other words, we are digging up fuels such as coal, oil, and natural gas and burning them in ways that release geologic carbon.

Here's a little exploration of government's potential role in the biofuels market.

A lot of people say using renewable fuels such as biodiesel or ethanol is crazy because those fuels contain a lot of carbon. As I explained midway through chapter 2, the difference is that the plants used to create biofuels and biodiesel contain *atmospheric* carbon, which was already in circulation, not *fossil* carbon, which comes new to the atmosphere from coal, oil, or natural gas.

But the formula isn't quite that simple. Looking at biofuels demands a life-cycle carbon analysis.

With biofuels such as ethanol and biodiesel, it is crucial to consider how much energy it requires to make them, and what kind of inputs (such as fertilizer and water, which both require energy and transportation) they need. Just as it takes massive amounts of energy to heat or chemically treat oil shale, tar sands, or coal to produce barrels of oil substitute, you can have biofuels that are energy-expensive, with a minimal (though desirable) benefit to climate protection.

For instance, biofuels that are fertilized by petrochemical-based fertilizers, that are maintained and transported by machinery that uses petroleum, that need more processing and produce piles of waste materials, and that require a lot of water might create only a small reduction in energy use and carbon emissions. When you add up all the energy and fossil fuel inputs, they could even be negative.

That's why it is important to consider the full fuel-cycle—what people call "well-to-wheels"—impact of new fuels. (That would be from the oil well to the drivetrain and wheels of your car.) If we are transporting a bunch of materials such as wood waste over hundreds of miles to get them to a biofuels refinery, we need to consider the energy that goes into the transportation, not just the clean energy that may emerge from the refining process.

Ethanol substitutes for gasoline. When ethanol exceeds 10 to 20 percent of your gasoline content, it can't be managed as gasoline because it is more corrosive and requires aluminum engine parts and plastic, not rubber, pipes and hoses in your engine and in distribution. It can even corrode the inside of a steel pipeline used for gasoline. This is one reason that some service station owners are reluctant to install ethanol pumps—they need new pumps, and they know that only a small percentage of cars ("flex-fuel" vehicles) are able to use gasoline with high concentrations of ethanol. That's why I work with service station owners to encourage them to install the infrastructure—pumps and tanks—that can handle ethanol. Sometimes they need incentives.

Diesel fuel, like gasoline, comes from petroleum. But the barriers to managing biodiesel are much lower than the barriers to using ethanol.

Clean diesel cars that can use 100 percent biofuels (even fuels produced in your own garden or back yard) have started to make a big comeback in recent years. These diesel engines are 20 to 30 percent more fuel-efficient than gasoline engines. In Europe, clean diesels are now about 50 percent of the passenger car market. The problems with old-style conventional diesels—noise and smoky, smelly exhaust—have been almost completely eliminated. An even-newer generation of clean diesels will hit the United States in the next couple of years—again marketed mostly by foreign automakers, in this case European—and will further reduce smoke and noise.

Diesels also have the advantage of using a broader variety of fuel types than gasoline-powered vehicles, and the energy requirements for refining diesel fuels are much lower. As I said, diesels can also run on 100 percent biodiesel and raw fuels, while even flex-fuel gasoline-engine cars that can accept ethanol usually need at least 15 percent gasoline. They operate at lower temperatures than gasoline engines as well, which can reduce air conditioning demand both inside the vehicle and, after the vehicle is parked in a garage attached to living space such as a house, in the house itself. When the new, even-cleaner diesels combine with hybrid (and eventually plug-in hybrid) technology, we could be looking at a highly efficient, zero-gasoline, zero-petroleum vehicle.

I believe the introduction and adoption of highly efficient cars—at least three times as efficient as Congress is calling for by 2020 in the energy package it is considering as I write—is an area in which the government, pushed by an aggressive president, can really help. So I won't just push for the low- and no-petroleum car, I will also push for a 50-mile-per-gallon fuel economy standard for conventionally fueled automobiles. People who drive them deserve cost savings just like everyone else. We can deliver that kind of performance—we know we can, because that is the kind of fuel economy being demanded in other countries and the European Union.

We need cars that get 100 miles per gallon, not just 35. We can do it with lighter materials and smart engines that use less power when they are up to full speed. These cars don't need to be any less safe, either. My friend Amory Lovins has shown how these cars are actually safer in most situations than the heavy cars we drive today. At a policy meeting I held in Santa Fe in December 2006, he took a carbon graphite composite sphere and challenged people to dent it by hammering it or throwing it or trying to run it over. The darned thing was impervious to any kind of damage we could think to try. Yes, it's more expensive than steel. But using it in more vehicles will bring the price down while saving lives and reducing insurance claims. Again, as so often, we can't consider just the original capital costs of these investments. Many energy-sensible ideas are more expensive at the beginning but save time, money, and energy over the long run.

The fact that individuals act in their own interests means that they sometimes take actions against the common interest. That is what has happened with energy consumption worldwide. The world's energy economy is built around technologies, resources, and private-sector players that specialize in developing and combusting fossil carbon energy reserves such as coal, oil, and natural gas. Our car culture depends on gasoline, and our electricity infrastructure depends too heavily on coal. As a result, the atmosphere is warming. We are bringing climate change on ourselves—much faster than we thought, according to a news report on the day I wrote this paragraph. It is in our common interest to adopt policies that push energy use toward more sustainable, renewable, nonpolluting technologies.

That will not happen on its own in an unregulated market. As we see today, individuals, companies, and nations will not choose slightly more expensive new technologies that reduce or eliminate greenhouse gas emissions, because they put themselves at a competitive disadvantage. This is the great weakness in President Bush's repeated statements that technology will address climate change (which he has only recently begun to acknowledge again as a potential threat). He's only halfway there. Technology is critical, but the adoption and deployment of the new technologies will not occur until there is some motivation for market players to use it.

It will not even happen at all unless the government uses its tools—fuel economy mandates, purchasing requirements for its own vehicles and buildings, rebates for purchases of highly efficient cars, renewable energy requirements, limits on carbon emissions—to shape the markets.

An exception to this are the companies that have decided, out of a marketing interest, a financial concern, or their shareholders' interest, to clean up their act. The companies that work with the Alliance to Save Energy, such as Dow Chemical, have produced climate-friendly energy policies. The American Gas Association and the Natural Resources Defense Council announced a collaborative efficiency policy when prices rose in 2003 and 2004.

Further, some individuals and businesses express their concern for the climate by deciding to buy green electricity or pay

179

extra for a very efficient car. The Sky Blue program offered by the Public Service Company of New Mexico (PNM), New Mexico's largest utility, offers different levels of wind power to businesses and households—up to 90 percent. I have put the state government totally behind these green energy programs, by any of the state's electricity providers, to help build their renewable energy market, even though these sources may cost a little more. Today PNM says that it has one of the most successful voluntary clean-electricity programs in the country. They sell perhaps 3 percent of their energy to Sky Blue customers.

Three percent? That's not very much! That means the other 97 percent of PNM's electricity is going out to customers who just want the basic service, mostly supported by conventional coal combustion. Because we have also adopted an aggressive renewable energy requirement for New Mexico utilities (20 percent by 2020), other customers will also get some renewable energy from their wall sockets. But the regulatory requirement of the renewable portfolio standard will dwarf the amount of renewable energy voluntarily purchased by New Mexico electric customers.

My friends at PNM kicked and screamed about the prospect of a renewable energy requirement for years, just as Detroit opposed seatbelts and fuel economy standards. It took a decade for a renewable portfolio standard to make it through the state legislature, partly because we had a new governor—me. Fortunately, PNM's management started seeing not only the environmental value of such a standard but also the economic value.

The wind power that PNM produces today is very cost-effective, and New Mexico (as I mentioned earlier) has a lot more that it could export to larger surrounding states and to energy-hungry, environmentally conscious states on the West Coast. PNM began to realize that it was sitting on a pile of potentially very valuable wind. That wind comes in at a predictable fuel cost, unlike natural gas or even coal. As natural gas prices spiked over recent winters, wind customers throughout our region found themselves price-protected and less constrained in their electricity and space heating uses. Wind's cost advantage made an economic argument for renewable energy development.

PNM hasn't liked another idea as well—the creation of a state or regional carbon cap that would force industry and utilities to buy rights to emit greenhouse gas pollution, at diminishing overall levels over time. But PNM has joined with a number of huge national companies, large utilities, and environmental groups to call for a national cap on carbon emissions. The companies involved in this United States Climate Action Program (USCAP) recognize that our energy consumption is causing climate damage, and they want to support new policy that will regulate emissions predictably and effectively.

I don't agree with everything the USCAP is suggesting as far as national climate policy—for instance, I think we should start with a market in which all affected pollution rights are auctioned rather than allotted. When you allot carbon allowances instead of auctioning them, you give them free to carbon users, perhaps in diminishing amounts over time. The price signal isn't there, and of course you open the door for people to lobby politically for a higher allotment than they need or deserve.

I say the system needs to be market-based, not political. Let the market, rather than influence or politics, rule. If we reduce the overall amount of permits to be issued at a predictable, gradual, but slightly increasing rate, business and industry will have time to prepare. Owners of large, inefficient operations might decide to retire older facilities and build new ones based on renewable, non-emitting energy sources. Other emitters might

181

decide to make retrofits that increase efficiency, and then they could sell some of their rights to other buyers who need them.

As I said in chapter 6, an auction-based cap and trade system makes sense. A similar system was included in the 1990 Clean Air Act amendments when I was in Congress—at the suggestion of a Republican president, George H. W. Bush, and EPA administrator, Bill Reilly. This system was aimed at reducing emissions that created acid rain in the northeastern United States. It basically reduced allowable emissions of sulfur and nitrogen and allowed emitters to compete for permits. That market-based cap and trade system has been an enormous success, quickly reducing these damaging emissions. The European Union, with California now allied, is also starting a cap and trade system, this one for greenhouse gas emissions. It began with too many allowances, instead of a real market competition to buy pollution rights, and took a year or two to settle down. But now there is some stability, and the market players can count on a pollution permit costing about twenty-five dollars per ton of carbon. As the amount of overall emissions allowed decreases in coming years, that price may rise somewhat. But people involved in the existing cap and trade program addressing acid rain have been surprised by how permit prices stayed affordable while emissions have sharply fallen.

So I favor using a market-based cap and trade system to start reducing overall industry and utility greenhouse gas emissions. It will set a high standard, then let the private sector decide how to best respond. It doesn't raise taxes or create general-purpose government revenues, but the auction proceeds will help support programs to encourage people to buy highly efficient cars and to implement energy productivity improvements from lightbulbs to insulation, and these revenues will help soften any price impacts that hurt low-income people.

Most people's eyes start to glaze over at phrases like "market-based cap and trade system." I understand that. When you hear that, though, what we're saying is that we'd like to charge companies for using up clean air, the same way they have to pay for electricity, steel, paper, or anything else they use when they make a new product.

That's only fair, right?

I also think we need to push the automakers to provide new consumer choices. Generally I don't want government in the business of choosing technologies. But in the electricity world, we are finding that one way to build renewable energy markets, reduce emissions, and provide predictability in fuel costs over time is through Renewable Portfolio Standards. It is time to push the auto industry to produce plug-in cars that run on electricity instead of on petroleum products such as gasoline and diesel. The automakers own the market, and they won't change without a push.

I wouldn't do this by a mandate or a standard, but my target would be to have these plug-in cars up to 50 percent of new car sales by 2020.

If we can fuel-switch half our auto and light truck market from all gasoline/diesel to 50 percent electric between 2013 and 2020, and combine that with a 50-mile-per-gallon average fuel economy for conventionally powered cars, we can save as much as 4 million barrels of oil every day. That's about 20 percent of our demand.

The auto industry will not start producing large numbers of plug-in vehicles without quite a presidential push. In fact, I would predict that they will offer the same kind of opposition that they have in the past to seatbelts and fuel economy standards—they will say consumers don't want it, the industry can't afford it, it will cost jobs, and it will raise the price of a car so that no one could afford it.

But every day that the Detroit automakers resist changing technologies and increasing fuel economy, they lose market share and jobs to other, more efficient producers. The trend has been going on for a while. Despite some profitable years, our U.S. automakers have been consolidating, falling behind, and struggling. Some of this is due to health care costs and other pressures, and as a nation we need to resolve the health care challenge. But there's a lot more to it.

American consumers deserve more choice, as well. I keep asking why consumers wouldn't love, *love*, a choice that saves them lots of money and means they never have to go to the gas station. As I said, no fill-ups, no tune-ups—only charge-ups. Americans deserve opportunities to reduce the cost of living and getting around. They deserve the predictability and simplicity offered by plug-in cars. They will have lots of cost incentives to buy plug-in vehicles. If Detroit doesn't offer them plug-in cars, someone else will.

I am happy that New Mexico is now home to a major electric car manufacturer, Tesla. This company will build cars for an upscale market, but as they get their cars into the marketplace they will also produce more affordable units for everyday folks. Like other automakers around the world that are exploring and deploying plug-in technology, Tesla poses a serious challenge, just over the horizon, to the conventional way of doing automotive business in the United States.

American automakers have a couple of choices. Baldly stated, they are: (1) resist technological change, rely on existing technology, and continue to bleed, slowly, at the expense of hundreds of thousands of jobs in vulnerable places from Michigan to Missouri; or (2) embrace change, work with the new administration, Congress, and auto workers to build a real shot at regaining market share and leadership for the U.S. auto industry.

Keeping plug-in cars off the market is not one of their choices, because other manufacturers will market these cars whether our automakers do or do not. In fact, existing auto giants will continue the trend of shutting down plants and laying off workers if they don't change. This technological opportunity is a life preserver, in fact a very nice and safe life raft, for a sinking American industry. The auto industry means a lot—a paycheck, an education, a pension—to many Americans. And just about all of us, whether we directly participate in auto production or not, are saddened when we see American automakers in decline, laying people off, closing factories, being leapfrogged by auto manufacturers from other countries. It doesn't have to be this way.

I would like Detroit to participate. I expect Detroit to participate. I expect Detroit to bust out of its "never, we can't" posture and do as it did in World War II, quickly providing the hardware this country needed to win a war. This time, the war is longer-term and mostly not military. It's a war on crippling oil dependence. And it doesn't require nearly as large a shift, nor one as fast, as World War II demanded.

We can help automakers face this challenge. We want to help startup American automakers as well, because they are bringing entrepreneurial ideas and useful products to market. And we won't freeze out foreign automakers—if we did, there wouldn't be incentive to make the serious changes we need to embrace. But the idea is for the Big Three (Chrysler, Ford, and GM) to be positive and excited about a new future, with help from the new administration and Congress.

I want automakers, utilities, labor, scientists, and the energy industry to come in and agree on a program for getting the plug-in car (all-electric and hybrid) onto the marketplace by 2013, with 50 percent market penetration by 2020.

We should offer large federally funded rebates for those who buy these cars, and the federal government should start buying this kind of car.

There are legitimate concerns about plug-in cars. The electricity we use today produces an enormous amount of carbon pollution. Gasoline has about half the carbon content of coal, and utilities that burn coal will need to burn more of it to produce the electricity demanded by plug-in cars.

That is, the utilities will have to burn more conventional coal *unless* we require them, through the cap and trade system I described a few pages back, to reduce carbon emissions overall.

At that point, as their allowed carbon emissions drop and as they see the plug-in car coming to market, they will start building low- and no-carbon generating options. Some of that new generation will be from renewables if we succeed at achieving a 30 percent renewable energy requirement by 2020. Some of it will be from other low-carbon options such as coal gasification, which creates methane or hydrogen fuels and separates most or all of the carbon from coal to be buried underground. Some of it could be new, safer nuclear power. The market, and regulators who watch over power generation and transmission, will decide.

The power of markets is immense. That is one of the great lessons—besides democracy and human rights—that the United States has taught the world over the past two centuries. The market has the power not only to create individual prosperity and growth, as conceived by that great first-ever modern economist, Adam Smith, but also to achieve big things for society as a whole. If we manage the carbon markets sensibly, with strict limits, smart incentives, and practical oversight—as we manage the

monetary supply via the Federal Reserve—we can foresee a
market-based economy that actually works toward *reducing*
pollution rather than increasing it. We can use the market to
provide consumers with new choices, while we also reduce
threats to the global climate.

We should embrace these market opportunities enthusiasti-
cally and optimistically. We don't need to create large federal
slush funds by raising carbon taxes and allowing federal agencies
to choose new research and technology options for study and
deployment. We can set an overall standard, auction pollution
rights, and let the markets move toward protecting the climate.
We can give Detroit and other automakers some support for new
technologies, and they will reverse their decades-long decline.

It's a positive, market-based way of addressing the twin threats
to our national security: global warming and oil dependence. It's
a new, integrated, comprehensive way of solving the biggest
threats to our prosperity and our world leadership since World
War II.

It's the first step toward leading by example.

In April 2005, when I was on my way to Washington to receive
a conservation award from the National Wildlife Federation
(NWF), I learned that the U.S. Senate Energy Committee had
just released a draft of its proposed energy bill—what became
the Energy Policy Act (EPAct) of 2005. I learned that the content
of that bill, in draft (true also of later drafts and the final bill
signed into law), was weak, doling out large subsidies to existing
fossil and nuclear players while continuing to provide only small
incentives for the creation of new alternatives and efficiency. My
friend Jeff Bingaman, then the ranking Democratic member of

a GOP-controlled committee, was still pushing for a national renewable portfolio standard, but even that sensible measure was later wiped out.

When I spoke to the NWF that evening, I took a few shots at Washington's abject failure to take bold steps that would address the nation's energy dependence and global warming contributions. The audience agreed, needless to say. The next morning I called Senator Pete Domenici, another New Mexican, who chaired the Energy Committee, and told him I had "given his bill a good whacking" at the NWF event. (He later became famous for a phone call with New Mexico U.S. District Attorney David Iglesias, who said that Domenici went quiet and hung up when he didn't get satisfactory answers about pursuing voter fraud cases against Democrats late in the 2004 election cycle. Well, Pete wasn't quiet when I told him what I had done with NWF.) He was so angry, and so loud, that I held the phone away from my ear while my staff and I listened. Pete is known for a volcanic temper, not just stony silences like the one that Iglesias experienced. What ensued was a press release from Domenici's office stating incorrectly that I had jumped the gun—there was no bill yet. My staff showed me the faxed and dated version from four hours before my speech, and I was able to prove that Senator Domenici had his facts wrong.

The minute-by-minute issue regarding who knew what when wasn't important. What was important was that Congress, instead of developing a bill that protected and advanced America's energy interests, developed another bill that was a set of compromises and negotiated agreements among dominant existing power players, from utilities and oil companies to auto manufacturers and chambers of commerce. That just isn't how energy policy—revolutionary energy policy that will lead the world—is going to come about.

Senators defending the utility industry recently used minority parliamentary procedures to prevent the Senate from even voting on Bingaman's renewable energy proposal. For years, Senator Bingaman has fought hard to require utilities to generate a significant percentage of their electricity from renewables because voluntary measures such as the production tax credit have had such little impact. The Senate's obduracy, despite Bingaman's leadership, is almost inconceivably absurd and a sad reminder that presidential leadership is nowhere to be found in resolving the energy and climate issues facing this country. If, as senators opposed to Bingaman's proposal say, mandates aren't needed and incentives will work, then why haven't our renewable energy incentives pushed wind and solar above 1 percent of our electricity supply? The new president will have to exert extraordinary leadership, with the support of Congress and the American people, and turn this entire energy situation in an entirely new direction—fast.

CHAPTER 9

Facing Reality

I n hitting the campaign trail, trying to convince other Americans we can follow New Mexico's example, I often talk about the New Realism. The current administration's lack of realism has led us to a dangerous place. We need to take a different path, one based on reality, not unilateralist illusions. As a nation, we must understand that the gravest dangers that threaten us today do not threaten only us—and that therefore to pursue our national interest and meet these challenges we must work with our friends, our enemies, and everyone in between. It will be a path not of hard words, but of hard work; a path of moral strength, not pious judgments. We will need strong diplomacy, backed by a strong military and by strong alliances. This is the path of American leadership.

Ideology and insularity have made a lot of policymakers in Washington believe that they can shape the world to their own beliefs. Some of this comes from a real commitment to bedrock American principles such as freedom and human rights, and I applaud that general interest. But mostly, the past seven years have been marked by delusion and a basic failure to ground ideas in reality.

I am proud of my record and experience in many areas, and I believe that what I have done on clean energy and climate in New Mexico during five years as governor will stand up against anyone's record anywhere. But every step of the way, I have checked and rechecked my strategies and goals. I know what is reasonable and realistic and what is beyond reasonable and realistic. Of course, my definition of "reasonable" is far beyond what most elected officials would ever commit to! That's because I believe that Americans aspire to greatness for our nation. They want to participate in problem-solving. They believe that we can lead the world in very positive ways.

And they know that once you say you're going to lead the world to a better future, you'd better pull out a map that shows the shortest navigable route there.

Unlike the great European and Asian powers of past centuries, ours is not an imperialistic culture or society. We are democratic and proud of it, and we usually respect other people's rights, not just our own. As Americans, we do not think we should conquer the world or take over other countries. Our greatest moments have been when we fought alongside our closest allies to secure freedom and resist oppression.

This is where the current administration has gone off the tracks. Many in the current administration think we're locked in an epic battle between the free Judeo-Christian West and the totalitarian Islamic East. The number of reasons this is too simplistic are many, but it is how some see things, and it has led the administration to describe the world as they see it, not how it really is. So President Bush, Vice President Cheney, and others exaggerated the probability and threat of nuclear weapons in Iraq. Later they cast the war against Saddam as a fight for freedom—a cynical gesture at best, since the United States has not involved itself nearly as deeply in other ground wars to remove tyrannical despots. And the administration has regularly, and wrongly, connected our enemies in Al Qaeda with Saddam's regime and with the insurgency in Iraq, which, despite some Al Qaeda opportunism, is largely a civil war among factions that have opposed each other for fourteen hundred years. These factions are influenced too heavily by outside Islamic nations that fear that the other side could gain advantage—and huge oil reserves—by winning in Iraq. There is a proxy war among different religious and nationalistic presences happening on the ground in Iraq.

Getting involved in that kind of situation—for reasons that were wrongly stated or overstated, without many allies, and on the illusory prospect of funding from native oil revenues—and then failing to manage reconstruction and rebuilding of the polity was unrealistic. If the old realism meant doing what was best for America without regard to morality, and neoconservatism means doing what some view as moral with no regard for reality, then I am proposing the New Realism.

The New Realism certainly stretches to fit energy and climate policy. We haven't been realistic about our oil dependence and our impacts on the climate. We haven't been realistic about the lack of competition and choice in our energy markets. The New Realism will present a different course, one that gauges the challenges and creates solutions that fit.

A few months after taking office, President Bush reversed on his commitments regarding regulating carbon emissions to slow and reverse global warming. Then he walked away from the international negotiating table on climate issues, deciding instead to start up an Asian technology-based partnership to deploy new energy technologies in fast-growing nations such as China and India.

But worse than representing a cynical reversal on a campaign commitment, the administration's failure to take climate change seriously was unrealistic, with consequences not as immediate as its unrealism in Iraq, but with the potential to change the very Earth we live on.

Scientists have confirmed, by increasing measures of certainty and in greater and greater numbers, that climate change is occurring, that it is probably a result of human action, and that emissions of greenhouse gases must be sharply reduced within the next ten years if we are to avoid disastrous impacts such as drought, disease, famine, sea-level rise, and severe weather patterns all over the globe.

Is it realistic to stand by and continue with business as usual in the face of these science-based facts? No, it's not realistic; it's ideological, politics-based decision-making that avoids necessary action. The Bush administration is saying, perhaps in defense of the existing energy structure and markets, that we cannot afford to change our energy practices, even at the risk of catastrophic climate change.

The fact that government scientists are being told to revise their findings or stay silent, and the fact that the White House staff has rewritten numerous government reports and communications on climate change, indicate that this was not an inadvertent avoidance of action. This administration has let precious years go by when we could have been deploying efficient new technologies, negotiating toward mandatory worldwide limits on greenhouse gas emissions, and building our energy independence.

What a waste of time and potential energy! A New Realist would say that we not only wasted years, we also missed huge opportunities. A New Realist recognizes that we can save hundreds of billions of dollars a year, circulate those dollars in our own economy instead of overseas, and create jobs and prosperity here at home. Instead, the current administration sees new energy policies as a threat.

America is an engine of global innovation and ingenuity. At America's colleges and universities, among its students and faculty, at its national laboratories, and in its most vigorous entrepreneurial and investment communities there is vital new enthusiasm for and commitment to meeting our energy and climate challenges. We have strong educational and research institutions. We have the world's best-trained intellectual and academic base. Scientists and technologists from around the world want to study and work here.

That is a huge strength, one that we must not waste and one that can nourish our growth and leadership in meeting the energy and climate challenge. Capitalizing on these assets, instead of running away in fear or protecting vested interests, would be the realistic approach.

In the past thirty years, we have grown overdependent on foreign oil again. Our energy efficiency is stagnant compared to what the Japanese and Europeans have done. We cut 17 percent of our oil dependence between 1977 and 1985, but since then our demand has surged. We just aren't being realistic about our own short- and long-term interests.

The New Realism should put away the political arguments against pieces of a new energy future. It should say to my friends in the automaking world, labor and ownership alike, "We can't afford to keep doing things as we have. We are losing market share, we are missing the opportunity to provide consumers with vehicles that use much cheaper fuel (electricity, for instance), and we are hemorrhaging jobs." It's time to take a different approach.

I am willing to do that. In my 2002 and 2006 campaigns for governor of New Mexico, I received hundreds of thousands of dollars in campaign contributions from industries and special interests that might have expected special treatment when I was elected. They discovered that I talk to everyone. I learn from them, and then I decide to do what I think is best for the people who elected me. Sometimes that doesn't sit well with people who expect value for campaign contributions—but it's a tenet of the New Realism.

The New Realism will not affect only political leaders and decision makers. It will affect everyday people. It will provide them with consumer choice: not just new types of vehicles, but new public transportation options (including high-speed inter-city rail and metro area transit), safer and more direct walking and bicycling routes, and communities that are more walkable and livable. But people make choices, and they will need to think about not only what choice is best for them, but also what is best for our country.

There's patriotism involved in the New Realism. It isn't necessarily a sacrifice, but it's a decision to try something new, to support incentives that might pay someone else a little bit more than you'll get yourself because of the timing of your own decisions, or because your circumstances are different.

Part of the New Realism is to recognize that decisions have

indirect, sometimes unintended or contradictory consequences. As we bring on electric cars, we need to make electricity supplies more climate-friendly. We need to consider how electric cars (like today's gasoline-electric hybrids when they are running on battery power) are so quiet that sightless people may be completely unaware of them as they step into a crosswalk. We need to think about how and where people plug in. We need to think about the materials and the space demanded by large batteries, including rare minerals whose supply is increasingly short. There are negative issues associated with plug-in cars, just as there are negative issues associated with the technologies we rely on today.

In other words, there is no such thing as a panacea, and choices have consequences. Every choice comes with implications and impacts. We just need to make the wisest choices under our circumstances. If we had been making wise choices all along, we wouldn't necessarily be so dependent on oil, and we wouldn't have ignored the probability of climate change in recent years. So it's time to get back to the basics, make wise decisions, and extricate ourselves from the corner we have been painted into.

When I was chairman of the Western Governors' Association (WGA), I tried to create a whole new direction for a group of states that had previously been dominated by conventional energy development interests. I am not out to persecute these folks, but I want to create competition and choice in energy markets, and sometimes that's not very popular in traditional oil and gas circles. As I said to Bob Gallagher, a friend and the head of the New Mexico Oil and Gas Association, when he came in to see me about New Mexico issues early in my first term as governor, "I will hear you out, but we're under new management." It was the same with the Western Governors' Association. My opening gambit was a West-wide clean-energy and energy-efficiency project—eventually the most comprehensive and largest project in WGA history—with Arnold Schwarzenegger, who had just been elected, which I described in chapter 3.

I wanted the WGA to be a major engine for wind, energy productivity, solar, geothermal, and transmission improvements. I worked closely with allies across the West, and especially in California (where there's strong interest in buying clean electricity, but there aren't adequate affordable renewable energy resources in that state to support a population near 40 million and growing). The rest of the West can help.

The most surprising result of the WGA project, for me, was the cost savings we could get from just the first set of energy efficiency investments.

As I said in chapter 3, we found that by 2020 we could save consumers $21 billion per year in the eighteen western states (now nineteen, as Oklahoma has joined the WGA) by efficiency investments with a benefit-cost ratio of 2.5 to 1. The same holds true for automotive technologies. Basic investments in efficient new technologies and fuel economy will save consumers hundreds and hundreds of billions of dollars, if only we can start making the switch.

Given the range of issues with our automotive technologies, which account for such a large portion of our oil demand every day, we'd be wise to be far more efficient.

Efficiency is the fastest and cheapest way to reduce energy demand, whether in electricity, building design, industry, or transportation. But often it costs a little bit more up front to save money and energy later. People with plenty of resources, a deep capital budget, knowledge of efficiency alternatives, and no quarterly spending report to corporate headquarters might choose to spend that small incremental cost of putting in more insulation, higher-quality windows, more efficient heating and cooling, or a new system to control lighting and temperature.

But since this section is about the New Realism, let's be realistic. Most people don't know a lot about efficiency. New compact fluorescent lightbulbs? OK, I'll try 'em! But what about a heating system that is connected up with some other houses, or an air conditioning system that includes underground ventilation to collect Earth's natural cooling? (This would be a system of underground pipes that circulate hot indoor air underground to cool it off during summer days and nights.) What about a home or business energy management system that reads all your current uses and turns lights off and temperatures down when there's no one in the building?

People sometimes need incentives to try new things, even obviously sensible things. So as we create a market for carbon emissions, and we require utilities and industries to gradually reduce their global warming pollution, we should put the revenue directly back into energy savings and new technologies. People who buy highly efficient cars, for instance, should get a hefty rebate. People and businesses that deploy efficient but more expensive technologies around their buildings should also receive some incentives.

Another aspect of the New Realism will be that regulation is needed in some cases to force the kind of energy changes we need. Fuel economy is a major area in which we have let vested interests stop needed progress. In 1985, as I mentioned, the Reagan administration actually rolled back fuel economy standards when a couple of Detroit automakers complained that they couldn't move quickly enough and consumers were being hurt. (Notably, Chrysler's Lee Iacocca never attacked these standards, and pointed out that rollbacks like the one by the Reagan administration actually hurt companies that had made the required investment to meet higher standards. To him, the federal government was unleveling the playing field in the interests of a few who wanted to change the rules.)

A few years later higher fuel economy standards were reinstated, but because light trucks, with a lower fuel economy standard, grew into a much larger percentage of sales, overall fuel economy stalled and actually declined for a few years. Huge sport utility vehicles aren't even included in some of these estimates because they outweigh light trucks covered by the standards. That is sort of ridiculous, especially when combined with tax incentives put in place by Detroit automaker representatives and protected by the Bush administration that give $25,000 tax credits for the purchase of one of these supergiant SUVs. In other words, we give out a much smaller tax incentive for some people to buy hybrid gasoline-electric cars, and then we wipe out the energy and climate savings, and a lot of federal revenue, by offering fat tax credits for monster SUVs.

That is about as contrary to the concept of the New Realism as you can get.

The world economy and marketplace—for energy, manufactured goods, materials, food, whatever—has grown much more vigorous and open in recent decades. This is a good thing. Generally, trade helps nations and people understand each other better. It opens doors to education and opportunity, not to mention prosperity, for people who might have expected little improvement in their lives a century or two ago.

Trade levels the economic playing field. That's why it is crucial to make sure our trade agreements require fair labor practices and basic environmental safeguards. Otherwise low-cost producers who exploit labor and the environment can undercut their competitors' prices.

If China can fairly make shirts cheaper than America, our textile mills suffer, but as with the auto industry, they are playing in an international market. As a nation, we'll need to make something we're better at making. But if the Chinese shirt is cheaper only because workers make sweatshop wages and owners pour chemicals into local rivers, we have to resist.

I'm not sure a lot of advocates of free trade understand the difference between free trade and fair trade. All goods cost something to make, and it matters what gets calculated in the cost, whether it's raw materials, human rights, defending oil transportation routes, or damage to the environment that needs to be cleaned up. Until all those things are factored in, you don't really have the true cost.

In the real world, there is no such thing as completely free trade. All trade needs to have regulatory oversight to prevent a cost-reduction competition to produce goods and services via the exploitation of people and the environment.

Trade also levels the playing field with respect to energy and climate practices. Unfortunately, the United States has chosen in the past six years not to participate in most of the international negotiations related to energy and climate, and the places where it has participated are slow-moving and ineffective.

During these dark days, we have begun to see what a race to the bottom looks like. Instead of trying to bridge the relatively small financial gap between doing it right for the climate and doing it terribly wrong, the Bush administration has said the costs are too high. It has done almost nothing to help steer fast-growing nations to deploy new technologies that capitalize on renewable energy and carbon capture. If the Bush administration's touted climate policies were effective, would China still be building one conventional coal plant after another? Or, for that matter, would we be considering about 140 new conventional coal plants here in the United States? The demonstration projects and high concepts are meaningless, overshadowed by the carbon continuing to belch into the atmosphere in increasing amounts.

Imagine a world in which atmospheric concentrations of greenhouse gases reach a level that seriously distorts weather patterns, temperature, and sea levels. Scientists say that level would be around 450 parts per million. We are at around 380 parts per million, up about 60 parts per million in the past century or so. By about 2020, we need to sharply curtail our combustion of fossil carbon-based fuels, globally, to stay under that 450 parts per million threshold that scientists predict could tip us into "catastrophic" climate change.

Climate change could make the world a vastly different place. That is a deeply human and moral issue, one that challenges us and provokes us to think about our relationship with our planet and its processes. It is also a fundamentally economic issue. This kind of climate change comes with a gigantic cost, the kind of cost I laid out in chapter 6.

Global warming could have a tremendously negative impact on the economy, a threat not everyone understands. Insurance companies have been among the first to recognize this. Jacques DuBois, who runs Swiss Re (the world's largest reinsurance company) and has a home in Santa Fe not far from my own, says that the costs of catastrophic climate change would run into the trillions and trillions of dollars. Huge investments would be lost, from homes and office buildings and bridges to ports and metro infrastructure such as water and sewer plants.

Other businesses are also worrying about the potential costs of catastrophic climate change. As I mentioned in chapter 8 when I discussed PNM in New Mexico, some of the largest companies in the United States have joined with environmental groups to call for a cap on greenhouse gas emissions. They know that the market dynamic—the cost competition that underlies our economic system—presses companies to avoid costs that they aren't required to bear, and that societal costs likely to be created by climate change are too great. The best way to avoid those costs is to create a system that makes pollution reduction a market imperative.

How much would it actually cost the world economy, and the American economy, to sharply reduce our dependence on oil and convert to carbon-clean energy sources and technologies?

There are trustworthy economic analyses from leading economists around the world (including a thorough one by Britain's Sir Nicholas Stern) that put the costs of converting to new energy technologies in the low single digits as a percentage of gross national product or of world economic activity. In other words, building windmills, using coal gasification, putting highly efficient cars on the roads, sequestering carbon, developing renewable fuels, implementing energy productivity measures—all these create a cost of 1 percent or at most 5 percent more than we are already paying. And it's not a tax. The reality is that it's a productivity investment.

This is one investment, however, that will pay off quickly. Within a relatively short number of years, those costs create net economic benefit. Even excluding the vast costs that could result if we allow catastrophic climate change to occur, we benefit by diversifying energy sources, creating energy in different places, and reducing transportation costs and the costs of defending oil sources and transportation routes.

Energy efficiency, or productivity, is a great example. I keep making the point that it creates a very quick return on investment. Today companies, households, schools, and governments might not make an investment in energy efficiency because it requires upfront capital for new lights or meters or motors, for instance. But those investments would be paid back sometimes as quickly as a couple of years, depending on the energy market. How do we help companies, households, schools, and governments make these small investments that are at least initially more expensive than the rising quarterly energy bill?

Right now, in the United States, we spend hundreds of millions of dollars every day to buy overseas oil. Our money is helping oil-rich countries triple their current account and trade surpluses into the trillions of dollars. Our money is supporting the gargantuan profits reported in the past few years by large oil companies. Further, even though the United States imports only a small fraction of its oil from the Persian Gulf, we spend as much as $100 billion annually defending the Gulf, and more protecting four or five other strategic oil transportation routes such as the Strait of Malacca, through which the vast majority of Indonesian oil is shipped.

We are already paying a huge cost for the existing infrastructure to develop and transport oil, as well huge costs to protect that infrastructure. Investing in alternatives will be a relatively small cost. In fact, once we start creating energy alternatives, we could dampen oil prices and help stabilize oil markets.

The New Realism will tie these ideas together into a comprehensive, aggressive energy and climate policy (laid out in the next chapter)—a policy that will at last serve America's real interests.

CHAPTER 10

2020 Vision: An Energy Revolution, in Five Simple Steps

I f you want pure policy, you can go to my Web site (www.richardsonforpresident.com) and see the latest version of my energy and climate policy program. I would appreciate your comments and ideas about the program, because I am constantly reviewing it and considering people's suggestions and comments.

What I want to do in this last chapter is something very different. I want to visualize what an intensive ten-year energy revolution would mean for us in America, for people around the world, and for future generations.

America desperately needs energy leadership. Our national security, our economic prosperity, our quality of life, even our atmosphere and our planet are at stake.

America can lead the world in new energy technologies, energy productivity, and the creation of stability in international energy markets. It will require commitment and participation by the American people, Congress, and the president, but it can be done. Indeed, with so much at stake, it must be done.

What will surprise us, as we proceed, is how the fearmongering about large costs was wrong. In fact, we will find out how much better off we are by creating competition and choice and by investing in home-grown sustainable energy alternatives instead of foreign oil.

We will also be surprised by how our freedom from overseas oil, and from the world oil market, allows us to pursue peace, human rights, and democracy across the globe — instead of pursuing and protecting oil.

I am not presenting an anti-oil program, but I am supporting strong new alternatives and the all-American, historically tested concepts of competition and choice, markets and growth.

As a nation, the United States of America has done big things before. As a nation, we know how to come together and solve problems. Energy security and global warming are huge challenges. We must address them boldly, and we must address them now.

My energy and climate policy, laid out in the goals and strategies below, is an integrated, comprehensive approach to a tremendous national challenge. It is not a laundry list or a grab bag but a set of strategic programs that work together to reduce oil demand and our carbon emissions. Unlike recent piecemeal efforts by the president and Congress, it creates a whole and practical response to a large set of problems. Instead of relying on the energy industry or lobbyists, it relies on American technology, patriotism, and cooperation. Instead of taking decades to produce results, it makes a sharp turn, quickly but safely.

What follows are the broad goals of my energy and climate policy, supported by the strategies and policies needed to achieve them. Every time you see the heading "2020 Vision," stop and imagine. It's a new America, an America of opportunity, optimism, prosperity, and promise. In fact, it's a new world, invigorated by America's example and leadership. It's America in 2020, after the energy revolution.

Goal 1

Reduce Oil Dependence by as Much as 50 Percent by 2020

Picture a world where we are not hostage to foreign regimes for 65 percent of our oil; where we don't ship billions of dollars from Americans' pockets to places like Nigeria, Venezuela, and Saudi Arabia to power our trucks and cars; where we pay less than the three-dollars-plus per gallon we do today to drive. Sound good? It's possible. But we have to break our oil addiction to get there.

I have written extensively in this book about the threats that have come over the horizon and are camped out on our front doorstep. I don't need to reiterate all of that. Instead, I want to paint a picture of the positive future we'll create when we reduce our oil consumption by 50 percent.

Our auto industry will lead the world again. Hundreds of thousands of autoworkers who feared for their jobs will instead work steadily and profitably, producing the new American plug-in cars that will dominate world markets in 2020.

Americans will live more comfortable lives, pay less for the transportation that eats up family budgets today, travel to schools and workplaces more safely and conveniently. Their houses will be warm in the winter, cool and pleasant in the summer.

Places like the Arctic National Wildlife Refuge, the Outer Continental Shelf, and New Mexico's Otero Mesa will remain ecologically viable and productive, untouched by the panicked last-second drilling of a society that couldn't discipline itself to leave something for future generations.

Oil price shocks from terrorism or supply disruptions? A thing of the past! Other nations, those still using too much oil, will suffer the consequences. We'll see much less impact on our economy,

211

because we aren't as reliant on oil. And because we helped slow down the demand for oil, international prices and supplies will be more stable.

Instead of consuming 21 million barrels of oil every day, in 2020 we are consuming about 10 million. Most of that comes from domestic sources and our neighbors, Canada and Mexico, whose economies have improved and with whom our relations are better than ever. And that daily consumption of petroleum is declining quickly because the trajectory of our energy policies is so positive.

Cutting oil consumption is like cutting taxes. Former Federal Reserve chairman Alan Greenspan likened foreign oil dependence to a tax on America's economy and consumers—a tax that is often paid to foreign nations while suppressing our own economic potential. No more! In 2020 we live without that hidden tax on our lives and our economy. And we have picked up almost a percentage point in gross national product growth by doing so.

By 2020, with hard work and the cooperation of Congress and the American people, we will reduce our oil dependence by at least 6 million barrels a day, probably 8 million, and possibly as much as 10 million.

2020 VISION

Promote plug-in cars

Close your eyes and imagine never going to the gas station again; never having a tune-up on your sensitive internal combustion engine—ever again. Paying a few dollars instead of fifteen to drive a hundred miles. Buying your plug-in car in 2015 or so, you might have received an $8,000 federal instant rebate—making it more affordable than a conventional car, and avoiding the wait until tax season for a tax credit you might not have been able to use. And every day, you save four to five dollars in fuel costs. By the end of the year, you've saved more than $1,000!

Is it better than going to Hawaii? Maybe not—but it might be the only way you ever get to visit Hawaii, by saving all that time, money, and aggravation.

This commitment to fuel-switching most of our automotive fleet is the biggest single step we can take. My goal is to make plug-ins 50 percent of auto sales by 2020. If we succeed, the plug-in car will save us as much as 2 million barrels of oil every day, with the promise of much larger savings as it replaces more and more of our fleet.

These new technologies work. The battery technologies that support plug-in cars and electric hybrids have come a long way. Investors and entrepreneurs are mastering battery technologies that will increase the car's range and reduce the size of its batteries in the short term, allowing us to aim for 5 percent market penetration by 2013.

There are two types of plug-in readily available (and affordable) in 2020: the pure plug-in that runs only on electricity from your wall sockets, and the electric/gasoline plug-in hybrid, which gives you more range and flexibility but is somewhat more expensive and requires more maintenance. Drivers choose between them based on which will serve them better (although some prefer to stay with a conventional gasoline or electric/gasoline hybrid engine.)

Imagine your satisfaction, the feeling of goodness, that comes with driving a plug-in car that not only saves you money but protects the world's climate. The plug-in car gives owners new flexibility to fight global warming. They can charge the cars from housetop solar or backyard wind generators. They can buy all-renewable power from their electric utilities. And because we require much more efficiency and renewable energy under this energy plan, while using cap and trade to retire older, less efficient generating plants, it is likely that the power coming out of your wall will produce far less climate impact than today's gasoline-powered cars.

213

Plug-in cars don't need a whole new refining and retailing infrastructure (as hydrogen cars, which have great potential for the more distant future, do). For plug-ins, the infrastructure is already here, in our wall sockets.

This program won't succeed without presidential leadership and the enthusiastic use of what President Teddy Roosevelt called "the bully pulpit." TR opened the Panama Canal, busted the trusts and monopolies that dominated American commerce, and set, for almost a century, the world record for handshaking in a day. (In fact, TR shook about 8,000 hands in a day. I broke that record in 2002, shaking more than 13,000 hands on a September day at the New Mexico State Fair.)

I plan to use the bully pulpit as no one has since the onset of the age of mass communication and the Internet. In February 2009, within thirty days of occupying the White House, I will hold a two-day No&Lo-Petroleum Summit with automakers, utilities, scientists, and labor. We will lock in a program to get the plug-in car on the market across the board and to make sure we are building clean electricity to fuel it. Visualize the evening news those two nights! Visualize the blogs humming with excitement about the new future we are going to create for ourselves—more convenient, more affordable, and more ecologically sustainable. And most important, visualize the plug-in cars rolling in and out of automakers' showrooms just a few years later.

2020 VISION
Increase fuel-economy standards for conventional cars to 50 miles per gallon

Admittedly, we might still lag behind Europe, Japan, even China in our fuel-economy standards in 2020. If so, that would be the saddest part of this vision, but it's proof that we aren't reaching for something unthinkable, contrary to the automakers' objections.

Let's say you are a person who, unfortunately, can't use a plug-in car because you often drive beyond its battery range, or because you park on the street or in a townhouse parking lot and you can't run an extension cord out your window.

But imagine this: because your conventionally fueled light truck or SUV gets 50 miles per gallon, you fill up only twice a month, instead of weekly. Gasoline prices have remained stable around four dollars a gallon since 2010 (or have declined) because we started reducing our demand so sharply, but you still save almost $100 a week! That's $5,000 a year! (Instead of Hawaii, you start thinking about taking a ride into outer space on Richard Branson's vegetable-oil-powered spaceship, which leaves the New Mexico Spaceport every day at noon.)

Gone are the self-pity and self-delusion of 2007, when automakers said they could achieve 35 miles per gallon only by cutting jobs. Gone is the view that lighter, more efficient cars are unsafe—in fact, they are much safer, because there's not as much dangerous metal and glass, and these new materials are much stronger. Far in the past are the wild projections that increasing fuel economy so significantly would add $6,000 to the price of a car—in fact, it's more like $2,000, and you make that back in less than a year of gasoline savings.

And voilà, we save another 2 to 3 million barrels of oil a day.

American pride is restored, as well. We're more like the America that cut its oil imports so sharply in the late 1970s and early 1980s. The great new technologies, materials, and alternatives we put into use from 2010 to 2020 result in an even greater and more rapid reduction in oil use than we achieved back then. We strip off the additional five hundred to a thousand pounds of extra weight added onto the average car from the mid-1980s through 2010.

In 2009 and 2010, my White House worked closely with automakers to ensure that this shift to more efficient cars was managed in a way that preserved jobs and promoted economic development. It required a coordinated effort between the federal government and industry to balance the range of public policy objectives that such a move entails—from jobs to technology development to incentives and public acceptance. Fortunately, I had spent my professional life weighing such interests. I support true public-private partnerships and recognize that if we are going to meet climate change objectives and reduce oil consumption, a close working relationship between the government and industry is essential. Cooperation will make these goals real.

Further, in 2020 automakers employ new engine efficiencies, including engines that reduce their displacement when operating at high speeds and ultra-clean, efficient diesels. Diesels save 20 to 30 percent in fuel consumption, can operate on 100 percent bio-fuels, and, as proven in Europe, can be built so they are quiet and smoke-free, compared to the diesels we knew in past decades.

2020 VISION

Reduce the carbon impact of our liquid fuels by 30 percent, and include 10 percent low-carbon renewable fuels in our liquid fuels supply

All those plug-in cars and the 50-miles-per-gallon fuel economy standard reduce global warming pollution from cars by about 40 percent, exceeding my expectations. (Combined with my market-based cap and trade program for industries and utilities, that means the nation has reduced carbon pollution by almost 30 percent in over just a decade!)

Wow! It's true! Leading by example works! Instead of building conventional cars, China and India have switched over a large part of their own auto industries to plug-ins and high-mileage cars, aided by the World Bank, G8 banks, and lending agencies. By setting an example and providing technology to other nations, America has started a worldwide trend toward carbon emission

216

reductions that looks as though we'll keep atmospheric carbon levels below the 450 parts per million dreaded by climate scientists.

You feel better about yourself. Your church is full of talk of stewardship enacted, not stewardship envisioned. You feel like a moral person—someone who cares about our planet and helps protect it. You remember seeing *An Inconvenient Truth* and being worried, quite worried. And you remember the energy and climate program that answered such questions as "What will we do to cut our carbon emissions so severely?" It was this one!

Furthermore, you see people working on local programs to turn agricultural wastes, wood wastes, and construction wastes into liquid fuels. They are harvesting switchgrass and converting it to liquid fuel by processes requiring only 10 percent of the energy produced—an even lower percentage of energy invested than was required to produce a gallon of gasoline from oil way back in 2007.

2020 VISION
Promote smart growth for cities and transportation

In 2020, weeks can pass without you needing your car. That alone saves a lot of money! Riding the commuter train that stops just five blocks away is so convenient—you can read, work on the Internet, sleep an extra thirty minutes. You bring your bike on board so you can make that easy ride across the business district, on a safe, dedicated bike trail, to your workplace. And because the federal government offers modest tax incentives for employers who provide shower facilities for employees, you actually sit down at your desk feeling refreshed, energetic, and exercised.

That might be the biggest difference between 2020 and 2007. You love getting to work! Pity the people who still get caught in traffic and waste hours each day!

Between 2010 and 2020, using Climate Challenge grants, we built some great dedicated bike trails between neighborhoods and around schools, so kids get to school on their bikes, the way they did fifty years ago. Those intervening years (remember carpools and the nonstop ferrying of kids here and there because you were so concerned for their safety on the roads?) are happily in the past.

Small businesses have grown up around the light rail stations: flower shops, bookstores, and restaurants that you can walk to and walk among. You see people you know. You ask for something and the owner knows where it is. Instead of driving to the grocery store twice a week, you pick up a bag of groceries every time you get off the train. The kids from the neighborhood who went off to college ten years ago? They are starting to move back. They like it here!

These measures that broadly encourage more public transportation and smart growth don't reduce oil consumption immediately, but by 2020 we see that they will sharply reduce oil demand in future years while improving our lifestyles and communities. They are indispensable in an integrated, long-term climate and energy policy.

Goal 2

Attain Efficiency and Renewables in Our Electricity and Natural Gas Markets

Picture a world where electricity is mostly renewable (that is, in 2040—we can't achieve "mostly" by 2020 because it takes so long to finance and change our electricity infrastructure) and in which you can generate a lot of your own. You didn't know what distributed generation was when I first mentioned it on *Larry King Live* in 2003, but today you know it is that reliable, safe, and saleable energy you can make from rooftop solar collectors.

All that electricity! And being used so much more efficiently! We use it to power many of our cars because we fuel-switched from gasoline. So we've conducted a serious campaign to produce more of it with far lower carbon emissions. We don't have as many conflicts about mountaintop removal coal mining in Appalachia, and the development of the Powder River Basin coal is happening at a much more reasonable and sustainable rate. When the National Research Council warned in 2007 that our coal reserves weren't as huge as projected, we paid attention, and we now use our fossil energy in balance with renewables.

That vision of becoming more sustainable, of building renewables so that they dominate the electricity markets and contribute to our transportation fuels, has redirected American energy policy. It's better for the planet, and the fuel (wind, solar, and geothermal) is free once you put in the investment to build the facility.

Additionally, we have started up systems to store wind and solar power, so they are deliverable when we need them, not just when nature produces them. Those systems include everything from compressed air in New Mexico's salt caverns to hydrogen at the windmill site. What a breakthrough for renewable energy! Just as I predicted when I spoke to the Federal Energy Regulatory Commission in December 2004.

2020 VISION
Attain 30 percent renewable electricity by 2020

Admittedly, this was the most difficult of all my goals for us to achieve. Why? Because the utility sector changes so slowly. Its plants represent a thirty- or forty- or fifty-year investment, unlike cars, where the fleet turns over almost completely every fifteen years. Some utilities don't have access to renewable energy. And wind and solar energy are intermittent and somewhat unpredictable, so developing systems to store their energy as nature provides it was integral to increasing the percentage of wind and solar above 20 to 25 percent.

But in 2020 it sure feels good to know that we're producing so much carbon-clean energy. The advertisements we saw back in 2007—the ones about a carbon-clean energy future by BP and General Electric—they seem to be coming true in ways we never predicted. It took mandates and federally supported trading systems for utilities that lacked renewable options, and it took investment in energy storage systems from coiled springs to compressed hot water to hydrogen, but we are finally turning the corner. It also required more federal support for grid-tied solar and wind systems, installed by homeowners and small businesses, that sell distributed energy back into the grid when their owners don't need it. It now seems more than realistic that we will meet the goal of 50 percent renewable energy by 2040.

Our large investment in efficient, large-capacity direct current transmission lines bringing wind from the Dakotas, Wyoming, and Montana into the Midwest turned out to be a huge saver for us. It means that Chicago, Cleveland, and some other Midwestern cities are now almost 100 percent renewable-powered. The large central solar farms in Arizona, Nevada, and New Mexico are providing similar amounts of power to California. We've really turned things around!

People in the utility sector said it couldn't be done. People selling nuclear and coal options said there'd be no room for anything other than renewables. People who know transmission and the condition of our transmission infrastructure ("the grid") said that it couldn't handle more than 20 to 25 percent wind and solar energy because they are so unpredictable compared to coal, nuclear, and geothermal energy.

But it turned out that requiring 30 percent renewables was the only way for us to get really serious about developing the bountiful sustainable energy that nature provides us in the United States. We stopped thinking that renewables were a niche response. Every energy source has its issues, but, in general, renewables create more energy with less impact than any other source. The world's strongest and most dynamic economy is now oriented to this kind of energy development and use.

2020 VISION
Improve energy efficiency by 20 percent

As my friend Ralph Cavanagh of the Natural Resources Defense Council used to say, "Customers pay bills, not rates." In other words, if you can keep overall consumption down, or even lower it, rates can rise and the consumer is not affected because he or she is reducing demand and use.

So in 2010, by federal law, we let utilities decouple their energy sales and efficiency services, and they ended up making a lot more money saving energy than selling it. In the process, we protected customers against rapid spikes in fuel prices. By consuming less, they were less vulnerable when natural gas prices shifted higher after the successful internationalization of natural gas markets by Gasport, the cartel formed by Russia, Iran, and others in 2010.

When I sponsored a North American Energy Summit in Albuquerque in 2004, one of my friends from Dow Chemical told me it was critical to reduce the growing use of natural gas to produce electricity. "Using natural gas to produce electricity is like washing your dishes with champagne," he said. He pointed out that fertilizer and chemical manufacturers around the United States were shutting down and moving their operations overseas partly because natural gas had become so expensive. By reducing demand for natural gas in the utilities sector since 2010, we have rebuilt the North American fertilizer and chemical industries.

We also implemented strict new green building codes with incentives for some extra investments. As a result, in 2020, new construction is almost 50 percent more efficient than it used to be.

In 2020 U.S. energy consumption per household is down to around 10,000 kilowatt hours per year, compared to 13,000 in 2007. We still have a long way to go before we reach the 7,000 typical of a Japanese household in 2020, but we might get there.

2020 VISION

Require carbon-clean investments for new power generation

By regulating that all new power plants had to be at least as clean as advanced natural gas starting when the law passed in 2010, we helped put an end to the proposed construction of new conventional coal plants. And this year, all new power plants must be 95 percent or more carbon-free.

We are gradually and predictably making the shift to a clean energy economy! It's something people thought they would never see only thirteen years ago.

It required a few more years of science and policy development to discover how to use all the carbon dioxide we capture from coal gasification facilities, but actually most of that carbon dioxide—injected into declining oil and gas fields right here in the United States—is helping enhance oil recovery and reduce our reliance on foreign oil.

We have definitely learned how integrated energy and climate policies need to be!

We have also learned that economists like Robert Samuelson of *Newsweek*, who say that climate-friendly policies are too expensive to be adopted in the marketplace, were wrong. The energy markets have benefited from competition and choice, as well as from government policies requiring carbon reductions and setting up carbon markets. As a society, we made a relatively small, sensible investment that has improved our economy *and* prevented the much higher price of climate change. We have proved that economics isn't just about the price of something today. It's also about shaping a sensible, affordable future. The technology was available—policy made it affordable.

Goal 3

Reduce Greenhouse Gas Emissions at Least 20 Percent by 2020, 50 Percent by 2030, 80 Percent by 2040, and 90 Percent by 2050

Picture a world where new energy technologies are creating prosperity and opportunity around the globe, many of those technologies sold by U.S. companies. Picture a world where the specter of global warming is no longer a front-page item because the United States has helped lead other nations to emissions reduction. And picture a world where the drought, sea-level rise, famine, dislocation, and ecological and economic disruption predicted by scientists have not occurred.

It's a much better world than the one we worried about.

When the savings proposed for the utility and industrial sectors through cap and trade were combined with savings in the transportation sector proposed under Goal 1 (reducing oil dependence by as much as 50 percent), we reduced greenhouse gas emissions overall by 30 percent or more by 2020.

In 2007, the United States produced 25 percent of the world's global warming pollution, even though we constituted only 5 percent of the world's population. If we included the carbon impacts of goods produced in other nations, such as China and India, that are bought by U.S. consumers, our contribution to world greenhouse gas pollution might rise as high as 50 percent, even with consideration of the carbon impacts of our own exports to other countries. (This number is courtesy of my friend Terry Tamminen.) We owed it to ourselves and to the rest of the world to sharply and quickly reduce our climate-changing emissions.

2020 VISION
*Implement a market-based cap and trade system to
reduce carbon emissions by utilities and industry*

In 2009, Congress passed my legislation creating a system to
ratchet down our carbon emissions by auctioning a declining
number of emissions permits to the bidders who most needed to
emit carbon. At first the reduction in annual carbon emissions was
2 percent, and in 2020 it increased to 3 percent compared to the
2009/2010 baseline. This gradual program allowed utilities and
industry time to observe the carbon markets and plan their own
reductions as appropriate to their finances and conditions. As a
result, there has been little price shock for energy users across the
country, even though they are now on a pathway to sharply
reduced carbon emissions. (Concerns about an economic recession or depression associated with proposals for an economy-wide
carbon tax, producing $50 billion per year as proposed by a candi-
date in the 2008 presidential elections, were averted.)

We used the proceeds from these carbon permit auctions to
pay for all kinds of energy efficiency and clean energy technology.
For instance, we are paying for weatherization and efficiency
investments in low-income homes, we are supporting tax credits
for solar and wind installations, we are funding rebates for plug-in
cars and energy-efficient appliances, and we are providing funds
for Climate Challenge block grants to cities and states.

This system, integrated internationally with other nations that
have adopted carbon limits, is also resulting in cost-efficient
energy decisions around the globe. Older, inefficient electric
plants that produce a lot of carbon emissions are being retired,
and new renewable energy systems are going up in their place.

Goal 4

Nurture and Invest in Science and Technology

Picture a world where America is the main engine of global innovation and ingenuity. The enthusiasm and optimism about meeting the energy challenges across the United States are inspiring—but they are also a valuable resource. We have strong educational and research institutions. We have the world's best-trained intellectual and academic base. Scientists and technologists from around the world want to study and work here. At America's colleges and universities, at its national laboratories, and among its most vigorous entrepreneurial and investment communities there is vital new enthusiasm and commitment to meeting our energy and climate challenges.

Actually, that is a picture of the world in 2007. Luckily, in the years leading up to 2020, we ramped up investment in research and technology and kept our leadership position, which seemed threatened by the politics of energy and climate change during the dark days of the early twenty-first century.

2020 VISION
Invest in a new energy and climate trust fund

This multibillion-dollar trust fund brings together public-private partnerships to make short- and medium-term investments. It researches technologies and opportunities that might not pay back as quickly as venture capital would like, such as hydrogen, the development of a national carbon dioxide pipeline network, or new facilities for refining biofuels. Further, it helps explore and advance new ideas that could scrub carbon from the atmosphere,

226

break through on new battery and energy storage technologies, or increase the efficiency of electricity transmission.

The trust fund is paid back and recapitalized as its ideas and projects succeed and there is return on its investments. It lends or buys equity worth about $5 billion to $10 billion every year, often taking ideas put forward by scientists and businesspeople associated with our national labs.

2020 VISION
Fund energy and climate research at universities and agencies

This program has helped thousands of graduate students in science, business, and engineering develop new concepts in energy efficiency and productivity, while also supporting new concepts in renewable and alternative energy. It is the breeding ground for new ideas that could create unexpected breakthroughs—ideas that sharply reduce energy demand or displace polluting energy sources in ways that policy could not have predicted. Many of these ideas turn into businesses that attract billions of dollars in investment— and help explain why, in 2020, clean energy has become the hub of a huge new cycle of economic development and investment in the United States, attracting more investment (and more *stable* investment) even than the high-tech wave of the 1990s.

Goal 5

Lead by Example

Picture a world united around the concepts of reversing climate change trends and reaching for a safe and secure energy future.

The United States is no longer the lone ranger. Instead, we lead the world by example—reducing our own voracious demand for oil, sharply cutting back on our greenhouse gas emissions, and working closely with allies in the G8 and the United Nations to implement energy and climate agreements that recognize our national interests and those of other nations.

The theory that climate change policy and economic growth are incompatible has been disproved by international oil markets that are more stable than they have been in decades, steady world economic growth, and a United States with entire new industries centered around efficiency and domestic clean energy. We have reduced our trade deficit significantly, and the dollar rides strong again, despite the horrible lows in 2007–2008.

In 2020 the United States is a beacon of the new energy future. Instead of fearing to enact good policy because it might not be matched by other nations, we instead adopt good policy and bring other nations on board.

In 2020 we have strong relations with Mexico and Canada, our major oil partners, we play a leading role in international negotiations limiting atmospheric carbon levels, and we help create multilateral defense strategies for major oil transportation routes (saving ourselves hundreds of billions of dollars).

Perhaps most important is what is *not* different in 2020.

There are no major suspensions of oil and gas deliveries owing to war or terrorist action. The same birds sing in the same trees, unaffected by the habitat creep many predicted with climate change. Glaciers and ice caps, while continuing to melt, are not disappearing before our eyes. Savage storm cycles, disease, famine, and drought are no longer predicted to change our very lives.

In other words, instead of worsening our oil addiction, we've broken it. Instead of avoiding our responsibility to clean up the planet and its climate, we've accepted and acted on it. Instead of behaving as though there were no future, we have respected the interests of future generations.

In the process, we have strengthened the economy, created jobs, and redirected and rebuilt America's future.

2020 VISION

Negotiate for mandatory international emissions limits

President Bush told the world in 2007 that he wanted to lead world negotiations that would, in eighteen months, produce voluntary measures to control climate change. Nobody really believed him. Even our closest allies, such as Britain and France, saw the president's proposal as a last-ditch gambit intended to slow down and derail mandates for change. We lost valuable time—on top of seven already terribly unproductive years. But in 2009 the new administration jumped in with both feet and the encouragement of our allies.

Wasn't it great to earn back the world's respect while addressing a huge global challenge?

We started with fast-track negotiations in 2009 that bound fast-developing nations to use energy-efficient renewable technologies with financial assistance from developed nations to help close the affordability gap between conventional technologies and the new ones that prevent climate damage.

In those fast-growing, populous nations, it has been difficult to get investors and local officials on the same page, but we have done so with the help of national governments, international aid agencies, and private enterprise.

As a result, we have taken the steps that scientists said must be taken by 2020 to begin reversing the threat of catastrophic climate change.

2020 VISION

Invigorate and motivate the North American Energy Council

The Richardson administration's North American Energy Council has stabilized the oil and gas trade, worked on a continental electrical grid, helped bring energy resources and productivity to market throughout the continent, and developed a regional system for carbon trading. The council didn't intervene in any nation's affairs, but it provided a forum to develop mutually acceptable policies for the adoption and approval of each nation's legislatures to accomplish several major purposes: (1) ensure long-term trade in petroleum and refined products, as well as natural gas, across borders in North America; (2) develop a continental electric grid, improving our nation's cooperation in energy and our ability to tap into cost-effective electricity resources throughout the continent, while improving management and standards across the board; (3) implement a regional carbon market, so that investments and efficiencies throughout a wider market will be represented in the energy choices made by all of our businesses, consumers, and governments; and (4) focus on development of promising continental renewable energy sources, matching energy sources with population centers that may lack such resources nearby. The council helped bring Arctic natural gas (from Alaska and Canada) to market. Further, by helping develop Mexico's renewable and conventional energy industries, the administration built a constructive, historic relationship with

Mexico that strengthened its economy and reduced immigration tensions.

2020 VISION
Finance developing nations to adopt low-carbon technologies and options

The Richardson administration has worked with allies, the European Union, and international finance agencies such as the World Bank to provide financing for developing nations to adopt carbon-clean options, such as renewables and gasification of coal, instead of conventional technologies that produce large amounts of global warming pollution.

In the process, we built international trade and strengthened American manufacturing. Nations that previously couldn't consider carbon-clean approaches because they were too expensive found themselves able to invest in stable, long-term domestic energy development, reducing tensions over oil and gas reserves worldwide.

In 2020, Americans are traveling the world again, welcomed by people who had grown suspicious of a nation they considered self-interested and arrogant. Today, as Americans help finance the energy development needed for growth and prosperity in the developing world, we are greeted with open arms—as liberators of hope, growth, and opportunity. And when we travel, Americans get more for their dollar. After years of difficulty, the dollar is back on top again.

Not only have we had these international successes in energy and climate, we have also improved international relations to such an extent that we are working with more than 140 nations to actively combat international terrorism. By working together on energy and climate, we produced a new atmosphere of trust and cooperation and reduced threats to Americans and their security.

2020 VISION

*Work to stabilize the defense of international oil
and gas transportation routes*

It took years and years of negotiation and planning, involving oil-producing nations, oil-consuming nations, the United Nations Security Council, multinational oil companies, and the world's economic leadership, but we produced a system by which the cost of defending the world's oil transportation infrastructure is no longer carried almost unilaterally by American taxpayers. The result: multilateral defense treaties that assure protection and cooperation, anticipate and address hostilities, and prevent terrorist attacks on oil infrastructure.

Now, in 2020, the system is beginning to work. Tensions in the Persian Gulf have never been lower since the first oil embargo in 1973–1974. Russian, British, Chinese, French, German and U.S. naval units share defense responsibilities according to an agreed schedule and system, with costs paid by those who benefit from the protection. Although Iran and Saudi Arabia remain at odds, they have established structures to work out differences and avoid confrontation in the Gulf. Iraq, unstable for many years, poses no threat in the region and has brought oil production and exports back to their prewar levels. Similar progress is reported in other regions of the world where large amounts of oil and gas are transported.

Stopping climate change and breaking our oil addiction represent distinct policy goals but share many of the same solutions. My portfolio of policy measures and investments is designed to aggressively—and simultaneously—address both objectives.

The United States needs to control its own energy destiny. Our reliance on oil undermines that possibility and distorts our foreign policy. This dependence—and the geographic and geologic distribution of the world's largest remaining oil reserves—limits our strategic options across the globe. Further, worldwide demand for oil is increasing dramatically. The competition for oil could force major alterations in the geopolitical landscape in ways that would be counter to U.S. interests.

The goals for the United States are simple: mitigate climate change and implement energy sustainability. The benefits will be many. Instead of exporting petrodollars, we will create jobs and energy choices for Americans. We will stimulate our economy with a new, sustained wave of investment and growth. We will save time and money in almost every American's daily life. Most of all, we will unite behind a crucial and constructive public purpose in our national interest. We will share a new patriotism and a new belief in what America can do when we join our intentions and efforts. As individuals we will share an important common purpose, and we will achieve benefits for every unit from households to large businesses.

The path to meeting these goals is difficult. It is easier, at least day-to-day, to keep letting energy markets work as they do. Successful navigation of this revolutionary path requires leadership, vision, courage, understanding, experience, and commitment. It requires the active participation of the president, Congress, and the American people, as well as our investment and business communities. I will bring these constituencies together to forge a new energy economy—an energy revolution—for the United States, and new opportunities for the United States to lead the world by example.

As I said in the first Democratic candidates' debate: on my first day as president I will begin bringing our nation's troops home from Iraq. On day two of my presidency, I will address energy. On day three, I will tackle climate issues.

My program and its 2020 impacts are a lot to envision. Yet we can achieve this vision by deciding as a nation that we must achieve it, just as we decided to enter and win World War II and to put a man on the Moon. This vision involves a nation determined to meet a challenge, in fact a threat, that drains its resources and endangers its national security, its economy, and the global environment.

It is just the kind of challenge Americans were born to address. We must act boldly, and we must act now.

ACKNOWLEDGMENTS

My first thanks and acknowledgments go to the people at John Wiley & Sons who made this book happen with the professionalism we expected—especially my editor, Eric Nelson.

Thanks also to Raphael Sagalyn, the agent who brought this book to fruition, sharing my vision for what needs to be said, as well as Howard Means, who got me in touch with Rafe.

Thanks to many of my friends, former staff, and advisors who have helped me develop my energy and climate policy for the 2008 presidential campaign: Rich Glick, Melanie Kenderdine, David Goldwyn, Ernie Moniz, Jim Baca, Gary Falle, Dan Reicher, Andy Athy, Bob Gallagher, Terry Tamminen, Laura Atkins, and Mike Telson. I know I am failing to mention many others, and I appreciate their assistance. Thanks also to Lee Witt on my wife Barbara's staff—always helping and always thinking ahead.

Thanks to Ted Halstead and Rachel White at the New America Foundation for giving me the forum to roll this program out at an event in Washington in May 2007.

I also appreciate the advice and education I received from friends in the energy industry as well as the environmental movement over the years. They are far too numerous for me to start listing, as I know listing any will offend others whom I forgot or didn't have room to acknowledge. Thanks to all of you.

Further thanks to the people on my campaign staff, helping make energy and climate a central issue not just for me, but for the rest of the presidential field. They include my campaign manager and friend, Dave Contarino, as well as Alexandra Sanchez, Amanda Cooper, Joaquin Guerra, Andrea Johnson, Mike Contarino, Richard Santos, Vicente Salazar, Janis Hartley and Sean Marcus, Pahl Shipley and Katie Roberts, Rick Minor and Eric Schnurer, my lawyers Jay Rosenblum and Paul Bardacke, and Steve Murphy and Mark Putnam.

I can't name all the local officials and legislators who have supported me as governor of New Mexico. As for agency staff and Cabinet secretaries, we are careful to separate their roles in government from my campaign. So I will simply thank them as a group for all they do to serve the people of New Mexico, and for the inspiration, advice, and hard work they have given me. Because he doesn't work for me, being an elected official in his own right, I do want to single out and recognize my friend and ally at New Mexico's Public Regulation Commission, Chairman Ben Ray Lujan, who's a genuine leader on energy and climate in the West.

And to Ned Farquhar, my former energy advisor, many thanks for his constructive, innovative roles in the campaign and my exciting years making New Mexico the "Clean Energy State," and for his hard work helping pull this book together. I couldn't have done it without him.

FURTHER READING

Leading by Example includes references and quotes from major newspaper stories and magazine articles from respected voices such as the *Wall Street Journal, The Economist*, the *New York Times*, and *Business Week*. Some of the major readings that have most influenced my policy on climate, energy, and national security include the following:

Climate Change Before he was elected to the vice presidency in 1993, Senator Al Gore wrote a compelling book on growing environmental challenges such as climate change. *Earth in the Balance: Ecology and the Human Spirit* (Boston: Houghton-Mifflin Co., 1992) recognized how pollution had grown not only larger and more international, but actually less visible, in the form of increased atmospheric carbon dioxide concentrations that pose little local threat (as would mercury, unsafe pesticides, contaminated water supplies, or soot). The vice president's later book and documentary on climate change (*An Inconvenient Truth: The Planetary Emergency of Global Warming and What We Can Do about It*, New York: Rodale, 2006) is an understandable, comprehensive presentation of the challenge of global warming—one that has received Academy Award recognition and should gain the former vice president a Nobel Peace Prize soon after the publication of *Leading by Example*.

Global Energy Diplomacy and international policy are weak points of the current White House, and—despite the hubris and military intervention that have drawn headlines (and international concern)—the United States faces tremendous challenges in restoring its position and influence internationally. In *Energy and Security: Toward a New Foreign Policy Strategy* (Jan H. Kalicki and David L. Goldwyn, editors, Washington, D.C.: Woodrow Wilson Center Press, and Baltimore: Johns Hopkins University Press, 2005), a variety of foreign policy experts analyze major energy challenges around the globe. I authored one of the forewords. Other excellent references on this topic include *New York Times* columnist Tom Friedman's many articles on energy and climate issues, as well as his book *The World Is Flat: A Brief History of the Twenty-First Century* (New York: Farrar, Straus and Giroux, 2005).

New Mexico and Western Policy on Climate and Energy A group of West Coast and southwestern states has initiated an aggressive regional economy–wide effort to reduce climate-changing carbon emissions (www.westernclimateinitiative.org). This effort started in early 2007 and is expected to conclude in late 2008. At my prompting, with California governor Arnold Schwarzenegger, the Western Governors' Association (WGA) adopted a comprehensive and practical blueprint for implementing strong new energy-efficiency programs (20 percent by 2020) and clean and renewable energy (30,000 megawatts by 2015). The report of the Clean and Diversified Energy Advisory Committee, as well as the climate and energy policies adopted by the WGA after completion of the report, are available on the WGA Web site (www.westgov.org). Important New Mexico references include the New Mexico Environment Department's comprehensive report on prospective climate change impacts that could affect water supplies, public health, habitat, and economic opportunity in New Mexico, as well as a report by the New Mexico State Engineer and my executive orders on climate change policy in New Mexico. These are available at www .nmenv.state.nm.us/cc/index.html.

Visionary Ideas and Policy I rely on a variety of policy advisors from my years in Washington, D.C., and as governor of New Mexico. Many of these advisors have not published their ideas and work, but three key references from past advisors are *Winning the Oil End Game: Innovation for Profits, Jobs, and Security* (Amory Lovins and others, Snowmass, CO: Rocky Mountain Institute, 2005), *The New Transit Town: Best Practices in Transit-*

Oriented Development (Hank Dittmar and Gloria Ohland, editors, Washington, D.C.: Island Press, 2005), and *Lives per Gallon: The True Cost of Our Oil Addiction* (Washington, D.C.: Island Press, 2006) by Governor Schwarzenegger's former energy advisor and chief of staff, Terry Tamminen, who has gone on to help multiple states toward strong new climate and energy policies. Hank Dittmar was a friend and advisor in Washington and New Mexico until he moved to England a couple of years ago to work for Prince Charles on architectural and planning issues. The McKinsey Global Institute's recent report on energy efficiency is a masterwork considering technological, international efficiency solutions that will save energy and help reduce global warming emissions ("Curbing Global Energy Demand Growth: The Energy Productivity Opportunity," www.mckinsey.com/mgi/publications/Curbing_Global_Energy /index.asp, 2007).

Business and Community American business is beginning to recognize not only that climate change is coming but that carbon emissions have hidden costs and that policy needs to change. To learn more about this, go to www.us-cap.org. These are international, influential businesses that form the very heart of world commerce. The Web site www.iclei.org/index.php?id=800 includes policies and ideas from more than five hundred cities around the world ("Cities for Climate Protection")— places that are innovating and changing from the grass roots up, places from which we can all learn. (I addressed this group in Salt Lake City and Sundance, Utah, in 2005.) Web sites for the American Wind Energy Association (www.awea.org), the American Public Transportation Association (www.apta.com), and similar organizations contain valuable policy reports and contacts for people interested in specific policy areas.

INDEX